Markets Without Magic

AEI STUDIES ON MEDICARE REFORM
Joseph Antos and Robert B. Helms
Series Editors

What ails Medicare is what ails health care in America. Medicare spending is growing substantially faster than we can afford, with potentially disastrous consequences for the federal budget. Worse, although the program is paying for more services, it is not necessarily providing better care for the elderly and the disabled. AEI's Studies on Medicare Reform is designed to examine the program's operation, consider alternative policy options, and develop a set of realistic proposals that could form the basis for reform legislation.

THE DIAGNOSIS AND TREATMENT OF MEDICARE
Andrew J. Rettenmaier and Thomas R. Saving

MARKETS WITHOUT MAGIC:
HOW COMPETITION MIGHT SAVE MEDICARE
Mark V. Pauly

Markets Without Magic

How Competition Might Save Medicare

Mark V. Pauly

The AEI Press

Publisher for the American Enterprise Institute

WASHINGTON, D.C.

Distributed to the Trade by National Book Network, 15200 NBN Way, Blue Ridge Summit, PA 17214. To order call toll free 1-800-462-6420 or 1-717-794-3800. For all other inquiries please contact the AEI Press, 1150 Seventeenth Street, N.W., Washington, D.C. 20036 or call 1-800-862-5801.

Library of Congress Cataloging-in-Publication Data

Pauly, Mark V., 1941–
  Markets without magic : how competition might save Medicare / Mark V. Pauly.
     p. cm.
Includes bibliographical references.
    ISBN 13: 978-0-8447-4261-8 (pbk.)
    ISBN-10: 0-8447-4261-9
    1. Medicare—Finance. 2. Medicare—Economic aspects.
3. Competition—United States. 4. Health care reform—United States.
I. Title.
    [DNLM: 1. Medicare—economics. 2. Economic Competition—United States. 3. Financing, Government—United States. 4. Health Care Reform—organization & administration—United States. 5. Insurance, Health—economics—United States. WT 31 P333m 2008]

    RA412.3.P39 2008
      368.38'200681—dc22

                                                          2008007010
12 11 10 09 08   1 2 3 4 5

Printed in the United States of America

Contents

Introduction

Medicare is consistently rated as one of the federal government's most valued programs. Seniors give it strong support, and even taxpayers generally favor it. This is surprising, given that it is a government-managed insurance program, with the government setting the prices for most of the services provided to beneficiaries. The surprise may be greatest for those who believe competitive markets generally do a better job of achieving productive efficiency and consumer satisfaction than government-run firms paying with government-administered prices. Given the popularity (up to this point) of the government administration model as compared to more market-based arrangements, what can we say about the choice between those two broad organizational forms for the Medicare of the future? Given its current structure, the costs of Medicare relative to the size of the economy are sure to rise, making questions about the performance of, and preferences for, today's system virtually inevitable. This monograph investigates whether greater use of competitive market-type arrangements might answer those questions.

Generally, I believe that unique (and favorable) financial circumstances in the past have been responsible for the relatively good performance of Medicare to date, which is why so many people have a positive view of the program. However, unavoidable changes in these circumstances will eventually make that model much less effective than market-based institutions. I argue that social health insurance for the elderly and disabled in anything like its current form cannot continue to function as it does now. Specifically, I argue that the effects of dramatic demographic changes, which will increase the

1

share of the population on Medicare, combined with a continued growth in medical costs driven by technology, will lead inevitably to a financial crisis if the conduct of the program stays as it is. There is no magic that can preserve Medicare as we know it today.

While limits to key financial aspects of the Medicare program are almost certainly unavoidable, I believe they would be best and least painfully implemented through market-based choices, rather than government direction. Not all is gloom and doom. The structure needed to make Medicare work well in this challenging future environment is one that relies largely on the availability of private insurance alternatives to the traditional government-managed Medicare fee-for-service insurance. This structure is, thankfully, already in place, tested, and functioning. The key policy decision here is a negative one: to avoid making changes that weaken the ability of private alternatives to survive and function. Policy should strengthen, not abolish, this structure, even at some short-run cost. Some elements of the current system (primarily applying to the traditional Medicare plan) need to be modified to do so, but the most important modification I advocate is a change in policy perspective that recognizes the substantial merit, and perhaps the necessity, of maintaining private options in the future world of constrained Medicare (and national health expenditure) budgets.

We do have much to be sober about. On the benefits side, the need for access to ever more effective medical care for seniors will continue to grow; its provision can be facilitated by a modified version of Medicare (and not by the traditional approach). But the financing side, whether measured by financial burdens on seniors or tax burdens on others, is bound to worsen. Market-based arrangements will make the best of this bad lot.

The ABC's (and D) of Medicare

Some background on the Medicare program is essential to the discussion ahead. A federal health insurance program for persons ages sixty-five and older, as well as some individuals with disabilities, Medicare covers over 43 million Americans and is expected to spend $475 billion in 2008. Medicare offers benefits under Part A (hospital insurance), Part B (supplementary medical insurance), Part C (Medicare Advantage program), and Part D (prescription drug coverage).

Part A. Medicare Part A helps pay for hospital visits, home health services, nursing facilities, and hospice care. It is funded by payroll taxes totaling 2.9 percent of total earnings (half paid by the employee and half by the employer). Individuals are entitled to coverage under Part A if they have a sufficient period of covered employment. Beneficiaries are subject to cost-sharing requirements, including an initial deductible for hospitalization (equal to the cost of the first day of care, or $1,024 in 2008) and coinsurance for long hospital stays or the use of nursing home care.

Part B. Medicare Part B covers physician and outpatient care, home health services, and preventive services. It is funded through beneficiary premiums (covering 25 percent of program costs) and a subsidy from general revenue (primarily the income tax, covering the remaining program costs). Although Part B is voluntary, most eligible individuals enroll in the program. The monthly premium in 2008 is $96.40 for beneficiaries with annual incomes up to $82,000 (for a single beneficiary, or double that for a couple), with higher-income beneficiaries paying a higher premium. Beneficiaries are subject to an annual deductible ($135 in 2008) and pay 20 percent of Medicare-approved charges for their care. Together, parts A and B comprise traditional Medicare.[1]

Part C, or Medicare Advantage. Medicare Advantage (MA) offers a private plan alternative to the traditional Medicare system. Beneficiaries can enroll in comprehensive, competing private health plans, including health maintenance organizations (HMOs), preferred provider organizations (PPOs), and private fee-for-service plans. These plans cover all Part A and Part B services, and they generally offer a prescription drug benefit under Part D. Medicare pays the plans based on a competitive bidding process; as of 2007, all plan payments are adjusted to reflect the health-risk profiles of their enrollees. About 8 million beneficiaries are enrolled in Medicare Advantage plans.

Part D. Medicare Part D is an optional outpatient prescription drug benefit, distributed through private plans. As with Part B, 25 percent of the cost of Part D is funded through beneficiary premiums, and the rest is paid through general tax revenues. Medicare's payments to individual plans and enrollee premiums under Part D are based on a bidding system. The average monthly premium was $25 in 2006. Part D plans are allowed to vary their benefits and coverage of specific drugs as long as the actuarial value of the benefit equals that of a standard plan. Many plans do not require an annual deductible, but all require that enrollees pay either a fixed dollar copayment or coinsurance that varies with the cost of the drug.

Demographics and Technology: The Financial Whole Is Worse than the Sum of the Parts

The problem with Medicare is, to put it simply, that its current financing is unsustainable, with two key trends interacting to produce a need for change. One is longstanding and roughly constant, going back to the birth of the program: Though not much different from the growth in private medical spending, the real growth in Medicare spending per beneficiary is quite high, and it shows no sign of slowing. In some fashion, the program must obtain more revenue per beneficiary, year after year.

The other trend represents a major prospective change: The future rate of growth in beneficiaries relative to the growth in the number of taxpayers, or the tax base, will be much higher than in the past. This is in marked contrast to the early years of Medicare (and Social Security), when both the ratio of beneficiaries to worker-taxpayers and the growth in that ratio were much lower than they are currently.

The basic conclusion is clear. The pairing of high real growth in spending per beneficiary with high growth in beneficiaries per

TABLE 1
ALTERNATIVE MEDICARE TAX-RATE SCENARIOS

Real growth in Medicare spending per non–means-tested beneficiary	2035 tax burden as percentage of GDP
Zero	2.6[a]
GDP + 1% (approx. 2.8%)	6.0[b]
Historical (4.7%)	10.2

SOURCE: Pauly 2004; calculations based on the Boards of Trustees, Federal Hospital Insurance and Federal Supplementary Medical Insurance Trust Funds 2004, table II-A-2.
NOTES: a = equivalent to 5.2 percent tax on payroll, assuming a constant ratio of taxable wages to gross domestic product (GDP); b = assumes that the GDP growth rate equals the "excess" Medicare population growth rate.

worker will be lethal to the Medicare program. Per-beneficiary financial needs will grow, while the population to pay for them will shrink (at least in relative terms). Either trend by itself could be accommodated by the current tax and administrative structure, but experiencing them together means that at least one component of that structure, and perhaps the entire program, has to be changed.

Table 1 provides some illustrative data on past rates of growth of Medicare spending and financing and the rates that are projected to occur based on current arrangements. To keep the taxes to finance Medicare close to current levels of 2–2.5 percent of gross domestic product (GDP), real growth in spending per beneficiary would have to be zero (row 1). If spending growth were at its historical real rates, the Medicare tax burden would more than triple (row 3). Even if spending growth could be reduced to a rate of GDP growth plus 1 percent (the estimates used by the Medicare trustees to project Medicare spending), the share would more than double (row 2).

The key question is whether the economy and the political system can sustain these kinds of tax increases. That is, the main problem in Medicare's future is not necessarily the growth in spending per se (because there are undoubted health benefits from some of that growth and equity reasons for subsidizing insurance for seniors), but rather the fact that about 90 percent of the program's spending is financed through taxation. I assume, as do many commentators (ranging from Alan Greenspan to Richard Lamm) that the answer to the tax financing question is negative: Medicare, in its current tax-financed form, simply cannot be sustained. So which features of the current form might be retained, and which could or should be changed? That is the question I set out to answer here.

1

A Voucher by Any Other Name

In 1982, Congress authorized new private plan options as alternatives to the traditional Medicare program under Part C. This program, implemented in 1985 and now called Medicare Advantage, was intended to promote efficiency by permitting beneficiaries to choose from competing private health plans—initially, health maintenance organizations, expanded to include a variety of other plan options today.

Since the creation of the HMO option, Medicare has operated what might best be thought of as a health insurance voucher program. Beneficiaries may choose among private insurance plans and cover the bulk of the premium with a subsidy of predetermined fixed dollar amount—in effect, a voucher. The vouchers are subject to some type of risk adjustment, with people needing more health care receiving a higher-value voucher. The vouchers can be used for a wide variety of insurance plans meeting a set of requirements regarding basic benefits and other operational issues. Those insurance plans can pay providers however they wish, can set whatever beneficiary premiums they wish, and can provide any benefits they wish in excess of the standard ones.

Before the prescription drug benefit (Part D) was made available in 2006, a beneficiary could choose either the traditional Medicare coverage for services included in parts A and B or a private plan under Medicare Advantage, with the total federal contribution being about the same in both cases (on a risk-adjusted basis). Until recently, the de facto voucher was supposed to represent an estimate of the cost of parts A and B services in the traditional plan,

7

reduced by 5 percent to reflect hoped-for efficiencies from the integrated delivery of health services.

Traditional Medicare is a defined-benefit program, in the sense that it guarantees payment for all medical services covered under parts A and B that are rendered to beneficiaries. In contrast, Medicare Advantage is a system of private plans financed as a defined-contribution plan (see box). In its most abstract form, this strategy defines a predetermined dollar amount of payment toward insurance, per beneficiary per year. It then permits the beneficiary to use that dollar amount as all or part of the premium for a variety of single-period coverages of medical expenses, constrained only to cover, broadly at least, the categories of care the traditional plan covers, with no higher copayments. Does this arrangement permit more market-like behavior, and has such behavior as it has permitted been found to be acceptable? These are the first questions to be addressed in this study.

The value of Medicare's private insurance voucher was, until recently, based on crudely risk-adjusted estimates of average cost in the traditional plan. Over time, risk adjustment has become more sophisticated, and the determination of the voucher amount has been affected by other constraints, such as payment floors for plans in "underserved" areas, intended largely to produce geographic equity (Medicare Payment Advisory Commission 2006). While the process for determining the uniform risk-adjusted amount has changed over the past two decades, it has remained a predetermined amount per beneficiary.

Prior to 1997, Medicare's payment to private plans was set equal to 95 percent of the cost under traditional Medicare of providing covered services, with rates determined on a county-by-county basis. This system encouraged the plans to operate in large urban areas, where costs under the traditional program were higher and high population density allowed for greater efficiency in delivering care. Plans generally did not enter rural counties because of lower payment levels and thinner markets. To encourage greater participation and give wider plan choices to beneficiaries in all areas, Congress included in the Balanced Budget Act of 1997 new

Defined Benefits, Defined Contributions, and Medicare

The traditional Medicare benefit plan, in parts A and B, was modeled after the Blue Cross and Blue Shield plans that dominated the health insurance markets of the 1960s. Those plans provided what are called "service benefits," meaning that benefits were stated in terms of entitlement to coverage for specific classes of medical services. Determination of reimbursement levels was also originally modeled on the Blue plans, paying hospitals on the basis of data about their costs and doctors on the basis of what they charged patients of other insurers. (Over time, traditional Medicare has retained the service benefits aspect but moved away from cost- or charge-based payments to a set of politically determined administered prices, with little or no scope for additional provider charges above the allowances because of limits on balance billing.) In health insurance discussions, a plan with this general type of coverage specification has been called a "defined-benefit" plan.

To avoid some confusion, I need to note that the same term—"defined benefit"—has also been used for public and private pension plans, and is to be contrasted with an alternative called "defined-contribution" pension. Though the words are the same, the meanings are different. A defined-benefit pension plan sets a worker's postretirement income at a dollar amount defined in terms of some measure linked to the person's pre-retirement wage. While the plan obviously does not specify what that wage will be when the person retires, it does promise to pay that amount regardless of the premiums the person paid into the pension over his or her working life and regardless of the level of earnings on investment of those premiums. If plan revenues are starting to look insufficient to cover the promised benefit, the plan might increase premiums or use employer assets to pay them. A defined-contribution

(continued on next page)

(continued from previous page)

pension plan, in contrast, fixes a premium contribution rate in advance (usually as a rate per dollar of wages) but specifies as benefits only what those contributions actually yield after investment.

Both defined-benefit and defined-contribution pension plans involve some risk. For the defined-benefit plan, the risk is premium variation during working lifetime. For the defined-contribution plan, the risk is that the yield on investment might be more or less than the level of retiree income the person might have been expecting when premiums were paid. For both kinds of plan, whatever the benefit paid on retirement, uncertainty remains about what prices will be for the products people will want to buy.

The term defined benefit in retirement insurance thus means something quite different from what it means in health insurance. If retirement insurance were "defined-benefit" in the same sense as health insurance, it would specify not a dollar benefit but a real "basket" of goods that retirees would get— so many square feet of housing, so many rounds on the golf course, steak so many times a week, and so forth. In this sense, there is less uncertainty in defined-benefit health plans than in defined-benefit retirement plans. A defined-contribution health plan, on the other hand, specifies a given dollar amount of average or expected expenditure per year, but not how much or what kinds of health care it will buy and, it is, paradoxically, really much more analogous to a defined-benefit pension plan, retaining as it does the uncertainty associated with prices, but committing to a specific dollar amount. Moreover, the distinction in private pension plans between postretirement benefits and preretirement premiums is lacking in Medicare, both because Part B is funded by current taxes and premiums, not by earlier payments, and because there is no necessary connection between an individual's Part A premiums and the amount of spending he or she is entitled to receive.

payment floors that were set higher than the cost of care under traditional Medicare.

The Medicare Modernization Act of 2003, which is best known for introducing a prescription drug benefit under Part D, changed the way the voucher amount is determined by introducing a type of bidding process for Medicare Advantage plans. For the present, I will continue to focus on Part A and Part B benefits, noting that the bidding process permits Medicare's contribution to some MA plans to be slightly less than the risk-adjusted, predetermined voucher amount (assuming that local payment floors are not binding).

Under the current process, an MA plan is required to submit a "bid" to Medicare, detailing its estimated monthly risk-adjusted cost for providing both Part A and Part B services to its beneficiaries. This value includes costs for services as well as administrative costs and profit.

The bid is compared to a county-specific "benchmark." The benchmark is set by Medicare to the larger of two amounts: either the Centers for Medicaid and Medicare Services (CMS) estimate of average local fee-for-service (FFS) Medicare costs, or the local benchmark from the previous year, updated for the national growth in overall Medicare spending or 2 percent, whichever is greater (Gold 2005). In many counties, the benchmark is higher than the cost of providing equivalent services through traditional Medicare.

If the plan's bid is less than the benchmark amount in the county or set of counties it serves, it will receive its bid, plus a "rebate" of 75 percent of the difference between its bid and the benchmark amount. The rebate must be used to provide extra benefits or to lower premiums paid by plan enrollees. If its bid is higher than the benchmark, the plan will receive the benchmark amount, and enrollees must pay an additional premium to cover the difference.

Under the bidding system, an individual choosing a lower-cost plan (one with a cost below the benchmark amount) recovers only seventy-five cents on the dollar of savings rather than ninety-five cents, as under the older administered-pricing system. For reasons I will discuss below, this change is unlikely to make a major difference in consumer behavior. Some similar and similarly modest administrative complexities arise for the new Part D.

These changes in the way the Medicare voucher amount is determined have led to a swing away from payment of slightly less to slightly more than traditional-plan cost. The Medicare Payment Advisory Commission (MedPAC) estimates that the private voucher is worth about 112 percent of the traditional-plan cost on average, while CMS puts the figure at 102.8 percent (for Part A and Part B services only). While the additional amount is not trivial, it is relatively small, is continuously debated and adjusted within a modest range, and is projected to fall over time. So let us continue to assume that Medicare Advantage remains a kind of de facto uniform-contribution voucher plan.

Closing the Circle on Medicare Vouchers and Markets

While Medicare has for a long time offered what is essentially a risk-adjusted voucher program for private (for-profit and not-for-profit) insurance options, it has treated the traditional government-managed fee-for-service insurance plan differently (though not consistently). When Medicare was first established in 1965 and the traditional plan was the only offering, it fulfilled a promise to copy the prevailing practices in private health insurance plans: Funds would be collected to cover the realized cost of whatever covered non-physician services patients receive, and physician services would be paid for at usual, reasonable, and customary rates. Over time, this promise eroded, as spending levels grew and reimbursement policy was changed to per-admission payments for inpatient care and resource-based, relative-value schedules for physician services. The overall rate of growth in spending was always politically controlled to some extent (by control of the conversion or update factor that translated pricing weights into dollars). The Balanced Budget Act of 1997 introduced the "sustainable growth rate" (SGR) formula, which sharply limits the growth of allowable physician fees. However, those limits have generally been ineffective. Scheduled reductions in fees under the SGR intended to slow Medicare physician spending have been overturned by Congress nearly every year.

In short, there is no doubt that even in the current setting the growth in funds to be made available for the care of traditionally insured beneficiaries is politically determined. The process of translating these political choices into payment rates in the traditional program is already awkward and unpredictable; in the future, with a greater need for limits, it can only become more difficult and more arbitrary.

The problem is that the traditional Medicare fee-for-service plan is nominally open-ended with regard to cost, agreeing to cover whatever patient and doctor choose (even though it has almost never been allowed to function this way). It is poorly suited to constraining spending in a fashion that will work well for beneficiaries. Almost the only device the traditional plan has for cost control (until the recent addition of some modest "pay for performance" schemes) has been its power over administered unit prices. While it apparently does have some monopsony power that allows it to limit or lower these prices to some extent, long-term spending control using only administered (and politically negotiated) unit prices is unlikely to work well.

As we will see, both political transparency and future economic reality strongly suggest that financing of the traditional plan should be converted as well into an explicit voucher with a prior and prespecified rate of growth, with the same rate of growth applied to beneficiary choices of private alternatives. We will also see that use of monopsony power to force prices below the competitive level in order to contain Medicare spending is likely to be both inefficient and unsustainable over time.

What Might Markets in Medicare Mean, and What Do They Need to Work?

Given that Medicare already allows people the option either to select the traditional Medicare insurance or to choose among a set of private plans that are funded through a tax-financed voucher plan, why all the fuss about competition and markets? No serious analyst advocates completely abolishing the Medicare program or the traditional plan. No one advocates turning the job of insuring older people's medical expenses entirely over to the private market with only private financing.

The real question is how to preserve Medicare's ability to achieve its goals of financial protection and access to effective medical care while at the same time securing some of the advantages that reasonably competitive markets provide. Since perfection is not to be expected in any realistic market, discovery of a possible defect is not necessarily a fatal flaw. The alternatives to market-based Medicare, even in the current environment and certainly in the future, are not perfect, either, since they also have gaps in protection and access. We need to compare realistic alternatives, not hypothetical perfection.

The first issue is defining Medicare's social objectives. As already noted, one goal is financial protection: It is reasonable for people to want to avoid even a small chance of a financially crippling medical bill. Of course, if a person with high use is to receive large dollar amounts of health care compensated by insurance, someone else must be paying in some fashion. In other words, beneficiaries must have paid a sizable insurance premium in the recent past, or taxpayers have to pay more; or assets accumulated in the past have to be drawn down. A second social objective of Medicare is to provide its beneficiaries with access to effective medical care, presumably at levels somewhat greater than they could afford if they had to pay entirely out of pocket or rely on private insurance.

How much financial protection and how much access to care should Medicare furnish? At least for the non-poor elderly, complete protection from all out-of-pocket spending and access to all care of positive marginal value, no matter how low that value is relative to its cost, is presumably not what society has in mind. There will have to be some judgment—necessarily imprecise because it is political and must deal with people with different preferences as voters and different needs as citizens—about how much protection is enough. Moreover, this judgment may depend on the cost of achieving each goal, and so may change when costs change.

The most we will be able to determine about any concrete policy is whether it seems to come close to fulfilling some notion of social adequacy; we will not be able to make precise judgments or program adjustments based on meaningless concepts such as "need" and "performance." To simplify the discussion, I will assume that there are no other social objectives for Medicare than providing financial protection and access to care. For example, I will not assume (or try to understand why others assume) that Medicare should achieve some kind of social solidarity, nor am I concerned about generational equity, fairness to medical providers, payments for the social safety net for the poor and young, or whether the supply of physicians is adequate.

So the question is: How can we meet the basic policy goals of providing financial protection and access to care? Can market-based mechanisms offer options that the current traditional program does not—and if so, how?

One essential element for market-type arrangements has already been discussed: determination of an appropriate, closed-end public contribution toward health insurance for the elderly and disabled. I will describe various ways of accomplishing this later, but the actual amount (within a broad range) need have little to do with how markets will work, as long as any excess can be cashed out, or individuals can use their own funds to supplement Medicare coverage, assuming changes in income have minimal impacts on the demand for health services.

The next element is the specification of minimum qualifications that insurance programs must meet to be eligible for the contribution. This description is usually rather general, and is tied to existing Medicare coverage and cost-sharing provisions in the traditional government-managed plan. I will argue later that an even less restrictive specification based on equivalent actuarial value may be preferable.

A third element is the option of having a government-run insurance plan; this is the case with parts A and B but not, at present, with Part D.

The fundamental competitive model can then best be described as a voucher program with the voucher amount set at the defined contribution and usable for any qualified plan, including the public plan, and one or more private plans. Conceptually, the voucher specifies a dollar amount and a minimum benefit package (in terms of cost-sharing and quality) for a qualified plan. Some suppliers may choose to offer benefits in excess of the minimum, possibly for an additional premium. Other plans may offer the same minimum benefits for less than the amount of the voucher, with the excess returned to beneficiaries in the form of lower premiums. The government is one among a number of suppliers of insurance options, but in the competitive model it has no special place or role to play.

From the beneficiary's perspective, beyond financing and the opportunity for choice, the only additional element required for this mechanism to achieve a good outcome is reasonably good information about what we may broadly term the "quality" of the coverage offered by different suppliers. I will discuss the complex question of what information beneficiaries need and can expect to get below. For the present, however, it is important to note that, as long as all qualified Medicare plans meet the minimum standards for social acceptability for the entire Medicare population, there can be no such thing as a beneficiary error from the social perspective. Medicare has not, as far as I know, ever approved a plan that would be expected to be harmful to or inadequate for beneficiaries.[1] In other words, regardless of the choice, the plan any eligible person picks will be one that meets the social objectives in terms of financial protection and access. It may not be the absolute best deal for the money, but it will be decent coverage. To the extent that the government performs its role as regulator of adequate plan quality well, the worst consequences of imperfect information can be prevented. No one will do badly in this quasi-market, although those who have better information or make better choices given their personal situations can do better than those who do not.

To be somewhat more concrete: Since 75 percent of the cost of parts B and D is paid by nonelderly taxpayers rather than the Medicare beneficiary himself,[2] taking this "voluntary" subsidized insurance is, for the great bulk of beneficiaries, better than declining it, even if a person does not manage to select exactly the best plan among all those on offer. And the regulation of private plan quality ensures that no insurance option will be seriously harmful to health or to financial protection. With that kind of a subsidy, and with adequate minimum quality standards, it is hard to lose; even picking a plan at random is virtually certain to be better than taking no Medicare coverage. Hence, the worst features of a generalized caveat emptor market can be avoided.

Some Unexpected Gold Stars for Competition in Medicare

Despite the appeal of the logic just outlined, the use of market arrangements in Medicare often generates opposition. I will deal with the specific criticisms later, but it is important to note here that even opponents and skeptics of market-based Medicare generally acknowledge that such arrangements can, in some ways, be beneficial.[3] One benefit, though grudgingly admitted, is that creating options seems to give some of the public something they want. Even if most will not choose an alternative to traditional Medicare, the safety-valve nature of having options seems to be of value. The key issue seems to be whether this benefit offsets opening the door to confusion or to its mirror image, adverse selection.

Also praised are the benefits actually offered by private Medicare plans, which are generally "better" in a financial sense than those of traditional Medicare (even if provider choice is limited). Sometimes this is attributed to overpayment, but sometimes credit is given to greater efficiency or sensitivity toward consumers among competitive private firms.

Finally, opponents recognize the intrinsic attractiveness of the fully integrated managed-care model, as opposed to the decentralized and uncoordinated fee-for-service model. The potential gain from full linkages of providers and financing (compared to fee-for-service government insurance combined with private Medigap) is impossible to deny, either from an economizing or quality-improvement standpoint. Moreover, it seems hard to imagine a way in which the traditional plan could be converted to this sort of arrangement. The addition of some disease-management programs may help, but the idea of limited numbers of restricted networks needing full-care coordination but skipping some congressional districts seems out of reach for traditional Medicare.

In sum, the Medicare program is already moving toward a more market-like arrangement, and benefits of that arrangement are accepted by opponents as well as advocates of that change. But are there still some serious defects? Alternatively, will such arrangements confer benefits in the future budget-constrained world that have yet to be noted? These questions will be addressed below.

2

What Can Go Right, and What Can Go Wrong?

Viewed this way, a market model for Medicare seems nearly foolproof from a societal perspective. Beneficiaries should seek out the plan that offers a given level of benefits for the lowest premium (or that offers the best benefits for a given premium). As they do so, beneficiary welfare and productive efficiency move toward the maximum, and costs move toward the minimum. Each beneficiary chooses the mix he or she likes best of premiums and generosity of benefits above the minimum, assuming any additional premium reflects the actual cost of additional benefits. Indeed, as long as insurance markets are competitive, even "overpayment" relative to some benchmark (a high value to the voucher) eventually shows up as better benefits for seniors, not permanently higher plan profits. There could be worse consequences of error in government management.

Probably the worst-case scenario (as a policy outcome) is if almost all people pick the public insurance. This would mean that creating the market option did not do any good; but it did not do any harm, either, relative to the benchmark of quality and protection offered by the public plan. Depending on your perspective, another bad scenario is if almost everyone picks a generous private plan because the benchmark voucher amount was set high; the inefficiency here is excessive generosity toward Medicare beneficiaries. But in the reasonably calibrated scenario, if many people do pick the private alternatives, they must judge themselves to be better off than with the public plan.

Either way, it seems, consumers can only benefit from a market-based Medicare option; at worst, it does no harm. And yet, market-type arrangements are often the object of intense criticism and skepticism, if not outright hostility. What do critics fear?

One potential class of errors arises from risk variation among the population, and it is based on two important premises: one, that because of imperfect risk adjustment, plans may fail to achieve the desired quality outcomes (in terms of protection and access); the other, that the cost to the government may be high. By "risk" here I mean expected expenses or benefits from a given benefit package, presumably related in part (though not necessarily entirely) to variations in health status; note that in some cases, a high-risk person may not be very risky in the sense of uncertainty of expense. For example, a person who has suffered a heart attack has predictably high health expenses for the rest of his life—a high-risk individual in terms of his average health spending. Someone who has not suffered an acute episode of illness but has genetic and behavioral risk factors (such as being a smoker) might have high health costs in the future, even though his current spending level is moderate.[1]

Skeptics of market arrangements fear that private plans won't provide access to adequate quality of care for higher-risk people; profit-seeking insurance companies might also design their plans to attract low-risk clients and avoid high-risk customers by stinting on care for the latter. Doing so either discourages high-risk customers from choosing the plan, or lowers the plan's cost if they do (although it may also open the plan up to bad public relations or lawsuits). To the extent that such shortfalls in quality or availability of services for higher risks are observed, however, they can be prevented by regulation. Any egregious maltreatment of high-risk people is fundamentally traceable to failures of government quality-assurance mechanisms. This stinting may occur in subtle ways, and the disincentive to engage in this sort of behavior will be related to any expected financial loss incurred by the penalties for stinting.

The other possible error—high cost to government—is the mirror image of this one. If some people are low-risk in ways the risk-adjustment mechanism fails to detect, plans in less competitive markets that sign them up may expect to make profits at the taxpayers' expense. In highly competitive environments, plans may attract low-risk consumers by providing them with additional medical benefits or low or even zero premiums. Either way, one might contend that an inappropriate group (plan owners or low-risks) is benefiting at the taxpayers' expense.

Both problems will be prevented or limited to the extent that contributions and insurance premiums received by the insurer are both appropriately risk-adjusted. Permitting an insurer to obtain a higher payment for a higher risk will eliminate the incentive to discriminate against high risks, and competition for the now-profitable higher-risk customers will eliminate stinting. Lower premiums for lower risks will diminish excessive profits and the incentive to overprovide them with beneficial but low-value care. If government can risk-adjust reasonably well (compared to what beneficiaries can predict), markets can work reasonably well.

Thus, this type of argument against market-like arrangements ultimately rests on an assumption that government is unable to perform the task of risk adjustment well. Since nothing in life is ever perfect, the assumption is surely true to some extent. It is, however, possible to guard against the adverse impact of mistakenly classifying some sickly person as a lower risk than he or she really is if one is willing to pay the price—that is, hedging our bets on the safer side of that equation. To be specific: It is quite unlikely that a truly high risk (as perceived by the beneficiary and an insurance plan) will look to the Medicare program like a low risk. The distinction that risk-adjustment methods may miss is between the somewhat sick and the really sick, not between sick and well. A solution, therefore, is to set the size of the adjustment for above-average risks somewhat higher than its estimated minimum for those individuals, to be on the safe side.[2]

For instance, suppose a set of people with certain higher values of observed characteristics were estimated to have a risk level 300 percent of the average, but it is feared that some in the set may be of even higher risk. Setting payment higher—at, say, the value for 400 percent—should avoid under-treatment (since the money will be there to pay for more care) or plan cream-skimming (since the payment amount will be enough to cover the cost of risks that are somewhat higher than they look to the program). In effect, by "souping up" the risk-based transfer to apparent high risks, the potential for harmful-to-health misclassification can be greatly mitigated, and the risk of being excessively generous to people who are classified as high risks but are somewhat less sick than the average in that class is one we could probably live with. There is some recent evidence (Lueck and Zhang 2006) that such generous risk adjustment is just what is happening under Medicare's new "special-needs" plans, which receive higher payments to care for patients with severe or chronically disabling conditions.

Information and Consumer Choice

Another thing that can go wrong with a market-based Medicare program is poor decision-making by beneficiaries because of imperfect information. I have already commented on the practical irrelevance of information to a beneficiary's most basic decision—whether to take all the parts of Medicare rather than no insurance. It is clear that everyone should choose a plan—but will they have the information they need to make a wise choice among the many different plan options?

First, consider the most obvious case of a typical beneficiary facing a number of different health-plan choices. (I will initially ignore any advantages traditional Medicare has in attracting enrollees that arise from its history as the sole initial option and its current status as the plan with a very large market share; instead, I assume that all plans have equal opportunities to attract enrollees.) If information could be near-perfect and beneficiaries all had excellent decision-making capabilities, they would, of course, pick the plan with the highest net benefits, depending on their viewpoint and preferences. This generally need not be the highest-quality plan or the one that leads to the highest-quality care, since benefits trade off against costs; it would be the one that delivers, for any given consumer, the best combination of costs and benefits.

By providing consumers with this choice and the information to choose wisely, the market will, in turn, reward plans that provide the most benefits for the money, in configurations that match what potential enrollees want. This would provide two good outcomes: cost minimization (given quality) and optimal quality (given cost). While even this blissful state might be strained as costs rise over time, as a general proposition, consumer choice coupled with really good consumer information provides a great many virtues.

While steps can always be taken to improve information, we obviously will never reach the stage where all seniors are perfectly informed about everything medical. So how much and what kind of information is good enough for a market solution to be net beneficial, compared to the alternative of a single, collectively chosen and managed government plan? Let's take this question one piece at a time.

The first point to make is that achieving the objective of cost or price minimization for a given quality level does not require everyone to have perfect information. Rather, as some deep economic theory shows, there need only be a critical mass of mobile buyers who are reasonably well-informed about the costs and quality levels of different outcomes, coupled with a reasonably large number of competitive suppliers (Wilde and Schwartz 1979).

Suppose, for example, that a seller of a health plan initially is charging the low price that just covers its costs, plus normal (market-level-competitive) profits, but is contemplating raising prices. It will generally be deterred from doing so even if the higher prices won't drive away all of its customers; all that is needed to make the price increase a losing proposition is for enough buyers who know this option is inferior to others to leave. A relatively small loss in the company's customer base might be enough to offset the added revenues generated by higher prices. The same response would be predicted should the seller be thinking about reducing the quality of its services to cut costs; informed buyers will leave, perhaps enough to discourage the thought.

How much is "enough" is hard to determine (and it depends on some subtle parameters), but the point here is that it is almost always well below 100 percent of all actual and potential buyers.[3] Moreover, the market discipline will be forced on sellers as long as buyers in this set know about some of the other alternatives; they need not know about all of them. So the message is that a cadre of reasonably well-informed buyers can be enough to bring about the productive efficiencies of competitive markets.

One important qualification: This is an argument about incentives at the margin. If the firm were to contemplate raising prices or cutting quality a great deal, driving away all but a small set of totally ignorant and immovable beneficiaries and then taking unlimited advantage of this stolid remnant, it might be able to make money. Plausibly, we assume that such a strategy would be easy to detect and easy to condemn (on both equity and efficiency grounds) and/or prevent.

The other aspect of a perfect market to consider is that buyers are all matched with the (economical) options that are present; for this task to be done perfectly, the information demands are much more severe. As already suggested, however, a combination of regulation and monitoring by the government mixed with some knowledgeable buyers can help to get pretty close to perfection. If I know what other people like me who are well-informed are choosing, I can just say, "I'll have what they are having," without the need to investigate in detail myself. And if, whatever I choose, prior regulation assures a fairly strong level of financial protection and access to high-quality care, slight mismatches that might reduce my personal well-being a little, relative to perfection, may be of small social concern.

In fact, when it comes to consumer information about medical plans, we have to be careful what we wish for. Making it too easy for potential customers who know well their own prospective health needs to discover which plans are best for those needs can lead to adverse selection, with some plans attracting a disproportionate share of high-cost enrollees. This will occur if (in a sense) the typical beneficiary becomes better informed than the administrator who is trying to do the risk adjustment. While an individual beneficiary gains from finding the plan that pays the most for his or her medical needs, the consequences of everyone's doing so may be to raise the total cost of all plans, and may therefore be undesirable. Ironically, what is best for the individual consumer may, in this case, be worse for all of us.

Parenthetically, the beneficiary lament associated with the first round of Part D benefits—"I can't tell which plan is best for me"—may actually represent a desirable situation if best means "best tailored to what care I am planning to use" as opposed to "best way of managing the overall processes of care for a population." In the short run, the lament was most likely due to the newness of Part D, but there certainly was government-approved information, presented in the form of web-based programs, that would allow beneficiaries to calculate which plan would provide the best coverage for the drugs they were likely to take—an engraved invitation to adverse selection if ever there was one. Regulations requiring all plans to offer a wide range of drugs would prevent the worst adverse selection, but helping beneficiaries to choose what is best for them would exacerbate it.

The Eight-Hundred-Pound Gorilla: Traditional Medicare and Buyer's Market Power

In an idealized conceptualization of an efficient Medicare market, there should be a level playing field. All competing plans, public or private, should face the same initial opportunities in terms of input prices they pay, access to beneficiaries, and brand recognition. But traditional Medicare probably enjoys an advantage over the new private options because of its familiarity to seniors and its large market share. That is, the history of Medicare has not been neutral; virtually the only option for many years was the fee-for-service, government-run traditional plan, endowed with an initial 100 percent market share. Its benefit provisions and payment levels were set by law rather than by business judgment, and its contracts (in contrast to private insurance) carried criminal penalties for violation. Whatever grip the traditional plan has on the hearts and minds of seniors, its large market share surely means that suppliers of medical services do not regard all Medicare plans as equal, but instead place more importance on the traditional plan. As a result, providers are more willing to accept price limits or even price cuts imposed by the traditional plan than similar reductions from a given private plan.

It would appear that, in contrast to almost all private plans, the natural economic way to describe the position of traditional Medicare is as a monopsony buyer, or at least a buyer with a lot of monopsony power. Other plans that offer less than the going rate of reimbursement for different types of care might expect few or no local area providers to accept their contracts. But traditional Medicare (in principle and in practice) can reduce its administered prices or offer lower-than-prevailing prices and still expect many suppliers to be willing to continue as Medicare-contracted firms and to supply services.

The extent of this power is not unlimited, and there is strong evidence that it varies across markets in anticipated ways. In most local markets, many independent physicians supply services; a fraction of them have always declined to take Medicare patients, and apparently more are refusing to do so over time (Medicare Payment Advisory Commission 2006). Moreover, medical ethics do permit a physician to pick and choose which patients to accept for treatment (though not abandon once accepted). Presumably, the reason a relatively small fraction of physicians refuses traditional Medicare patients is that many others not covered by Medicare can substitute for them, and might be attracted by small changes in price or quality. In contrast, virtually all hospitals accept all Medicare patients and are willing to take more at the price Medicare pays. Hospitals have few tools for picking and choosing patients; generally, they must be open to all, and their ability to replace what is usually a large fraction of their business is limited by the small number of other competitors from whom they can attract customers.

However, while traditional Medicare has potential market power, it seems thus far not to have used it as fully as the conventional monopsonist in economic theory. The conventional monopsonist pushes supplier price down by curtailing its purchases. In a monopsony equilibrium, quantity—in this case, based on a reduction in the number of health-care providers willing to accept Medicare patients—is less than in the competitive setting, and no supplier is willing to supply more than it is currently supplying at the prevailing price. But until recently, despite some exceptions, most physicians accepted Medicare patients, and the fraction of beneficiaries who reported problems in access was quite small; this is not consistent with monopsony. And hospitals remain willing to accept additional patients and supply more services. It does not appear that Medicare has followed the traditional strategy of forcing down the quantity of health services in order to pay a lower price; things may be changing somewhat for physician services, but even here the volume of services has increased rather than fallen over time even as some physicians decline new Medicare patients.

Rather than acting as the traditional cost-minimizing monopsonist, if traditional Medicare has imposed lower prices, it has done so without an offsetting reduction in quantity. Instead of an account of movement from competitive price levels to monopsony ones, the story seems to be much more one of movement from initial overpayment when Medicare was first set up—evidenced by excessive willingness of doctors and hospitals to supply at the margin—to less overpayment. This apparently resulted from the 1997 Balanced Budget Act, which depressed both hospital and physician payments below trend. Traditional Medicare was able to retain access at lower prices to almost all providers, unlike competing private plans.

Though somewhat complicated by quantity offsets by some physicians and the apparent recent lessening of physicians' willingness to take Medicare, the overall pattern is much more consistent with *political* power than with economic monopsony power. That is, hospitals surely were reluctant to turn away Medicare patients when payments were constrained, even if it made business sense to do so; and possibly many physicians were fearful as well, because of worries about looking bad and generating ill will among the people in their communities. Medical ethics doubtless reinforced this behavior.

This observation leads us to a hypothesis: Traditional Medicare has political power it can exercise to support pricing policies that a private insurer with an equivalent market share could never dream of using. My judgment is that traditional Medicare has, indeed, had this power; the key policy questions are how much power it has had, and whether allowing it to be exercised is socially desirable.

On the question of the extent of its power, there is some evidence that, like Medicaid, traditional Medicare faces some limitations on its ability to force down prices without repercussions. Cracks are developing in the payment systems for physicians especially. Legislated payment-rate reductions for physicians under the "sustainable growth rate" formula have proved to be politically unacceptable, placing pressure on Congress to find a way to void scheduled reductions despite the increasing cost to the federal budget. I do not anticipate that further price constraint by traditional Medicare would cause suppliers (especially hospitals) to desert in droves, but it does seem likely that, having priced above its supply curve for many years, traditional Medicare is pushing it and is starting to experience adverse side effects of lower prices.

The normative evaluation of such clout-based pricing is not obvious. Monopsony is inefficient because it depresses quantity and quality, but so far traditional Medicare appears largely to have avoided quantity effects, and no one knows about quality. Lower provider net revenues per se may have three impacts. First, nonprofit hospitals that previously priced private business below the profit-maximizing level may raise their prices, and, second, some providers may exit the market, and consequently drive up prices of those that remain regardless of ownership type. The strongest effect is a wealth transfer from physicians (and even specialized hospital workers, such as nurses) to government and ultimately to taxpayers and beneficiaries; we are all conspiring to impoverish our physicians. The main downside of this type of raw bargaining power, however, is that it can permit the holder of it to be inefficient in many other ways and actually incur higher true costs than other competitors, and to cover up those inefficiencies by the transfers extracted from providers.

3

How Many Plans?

So far, we have examined what is needed to produce good outcomes for a set of beneficiaries choosing among a range of insurance plans. How many and what types of plans would be both best and feasible? There are two kinds of answers to this question.

First, to the extent that beneficiaries differ in their preferences for insurance (something I will expand upon below), there should be at least enough *different* plans to allow reasonably close matching of consumer preferences and plans.

Second, for each type of plan, there should be enough options to allow the competitive pressures discussed above to be meaningful. This definitely means more than one plan (monopoly), or even two, where plans may strategize to the disadvantage of consumers. Some economic models of conventional markets suggest that four or five reasonably robust sellers of a given product may be enough to discipline markets when prices are set in the usual way (Bresnahan and Reiss 1991). The current bidding process tied to benchmarks (as discussed earlier) probably strengthens competitive pressures as well, both by improving transparency and by fostering potential entry by allowing an insurance provider to propose a low-priced plan without actually having to go ahead with it if other bids make it less cost-effective.[1]

To the extent that establishing a new health plan has fixed costs (as it surely does), the number of sellers ought to be consistent with cost minimization. A less populous market, only large enough to accommodate two or three plans of optimal size, should probably not have many more actual offerings, at least not in the long run. This would not preclude there being many firms at first, with the competitive process winnowing the numbers down.

Can too many firms cause confusion—a charge leveled against the private Part D plans? Clearly, if people say they are confused, they probably are. But there is no getting around the fact that, no matter what, choosing health insurance is going to strain the mind, if only because people are being asked to make choices about new and risky situations where estimating and assessing the odds is bound to leave uncertainty. Even if I were the most brilliant and superbly well-informed Medicare actuary-statistician, I still might choose a plan that (even if it seemed optimal when I chose it, taking into account all the possible things that could happen to me) might turn out to be inferior to the absolute best plan I could have chosen with the benefit of perfect foresight.

Confusion is inevitable whenever there is choice about insurance. So the real policy questions are, should there be choice, and, if so, are there ways to structure choices so they are both less confusing *and* lead to better outcomes?

Market-based arrangements answer the first question by definition: In such arrangements, there must be choice. Implicit to this argument is that having many plans will be better than having a single plan chosen and run by the government. You either accept this premise, or you do not; here I will assume that you do (at least for the sake of argument). I will return to this larger issue below.

One way to approach the second question is to think about benefits and costs of alternative ways of structuring and presenting choices. Key issues here are the number of plans, whether there should be a government plan as well as private plans to choose from, what the fallback or default option will be for beneficiaries, when a person should have to commit to a plan and for how long, and the ways by which the government and the plans themselves (or some other agent, such as a nonprofit organization) might provide information.

With regard to numbers and types of plans, there are two opposing forces. On the one hand, having more options to explore generally raises the "costs" (broadly defined) to consumers making the choice. That is, at least if the person wants to be informed to a certain level about each plan option, more options mean more effort. On the other hand, having more choices improves the matching of the population to plans with characteristics (for the money) that they prefer.[2]

To address this policy dilemma, plans should be added to the market as long as the increase in total search costs is less than the increase in the value of better matches. If people differ little in their preferences, the ideal number of options will be low; but if people are efficient and have low costs from searching, the ideal number of options will be higher. On an abstract level, the truth of that proposition seems self-evident; putting it into practice, however, may be more difficult.

To my knowledge, there are no data that would fill out this qualitative observation. What's more, no general theory would argue that open, unregulated markets would necessarily lead to the right number of options; the numbers could be too many or too few. Hence the dilemma: We do not know if the market outcome is right, but we do not have the data to correct it if it is not; we do not even know which direction (more options, fewer options) is an improvement.

One general strategy for improvement is to make sure the choices include at least one plan that provides a good "safe harbor" for the average beneficiary. Those people for whom choice is especially costly or stressful should be directed toward this plan which, though perhaps not the best of all possible choices, at least won't be too bad. This safe harbor might well be a public plan with a moderate market share, for those who are more prone to trust collective choice and government management than their own personal choice or the tender mercies of capitalism. If high subjective search costs and trust in the government are positively correlated, a single public plan can do double duty. Related to this, the safe harbor should also be a fallback or default option, which is not "no plan," but is one of the choices. Research shows that people generally gravitate to whatever is the default option even when other options are present (Madrian and Shea 2001); selecting one or more pretty good plans as the default option therefore may be important.

For those who prefer a public option for coverage of hospitalization, physician visits, and other health-care services, Medicare parts A and B currently offer one (although, as noted above, traditional Medicare's large market share generates concern about monopsony). Part D in its current form has only private options. For precisely that reason, there is no politically acceptable rationale for choosing one plan or a subset of plans as a default option or a safe harbor for prescription drug coverage; the government (in contrast to a private employer) is required to treat all insurance options fairly and alike. So should there have been (or should there be) a government-run Medicare Part D option? The tradeoff here is the danger that if too many people choose or are slotted into the government fallback plan, that plan may have (and make use of) monopsony power in its dealings with suppliers, and will have pride of place in the political process. Some people think that public-sector bargaining power is a good thing, and indeed it may be from a distributional point of view; but it probably is not from an efficiency point of view. I will expand on this point below.

The next question is: How long should a beneficiary be required to commit to a plan choice? The length of time a plan can expect to retain an enrollee (even one who quickly becomes dissatisfied with his current choice) affects both risk-selection and information-gathering. It should be clear (though it not always is) that it is undesirable to permit people to switch insurance plans on a moment's notice or wait until the last minute to sign up with a plan when the occurrence of an illness makes a new benefit package more attractive. To prevent adverse selection, one cannot allow people to move instantly to the option that turns out to be best for them, because then the cost of that option will rise so high as to be financially unsustainable. Requiring a time commitment in advance should increase the incentives to make good choices in the first place. It follows that plans should, in turn, also be required to make commitments for key dimensions of their coverage policy (such as which drugs are preferred) for the same time period. Doing so will inhibit the possibility of negotiating some good bargains on pharmaceuticals with drug companies, but such bargains are unlikely to yield serious efficiency gains, anyway.

Addressing our final point about alternative ways of structuring and presenting choices, how might the government and the plans themselves go about supplying information to beneficiaries? Information is a public good, which means that developing information for one consumer can be quite costly, but the marginal cost of providing that information to additional users is quite low. At least in theory, the problem is clear: Because the cost of disseminating information is much lower than the cost of producing it for the "first copy" of a data report, information may be undersupplied in markets. However, empirical evidence for other insurance programs offering a variety of plan choices indicates that it is feasible for the private sector to supply much useful information.[3]

Despite its role in financing, the government itself seems unsuited to be a *producer* of information, both because it has no technical advantage over private firms in doing so (above and beyond the power to order plans and beneficiaries to provide data), and because political considerations limit its ability to provide information that places some plans at a disadvantage to others, especially when (as is often the case) the information is suggestive but not conclusive. For example, President George W. Bush ordered Medicare to divulge how much it pays hospitals, but such information is probably not very useful, either for private plans or for private citizens. Moreover, providing valid but imperfect information is usually not fair, as there is a random element in any practical rating scheme that will sometimes penalize the decent performer (or give the below-par a break); the restaurant visited by the critic on the chef's night off, for instance, may be given a low rating even though it is fairly good. As long as errors are moderate and random, consumers can still make good choices, but the arrangement will look unfair to the unlucky suppliers. They will have to deal with reality.

One strategy would be to solve the problem of information as public goods by using tax funding to pay for beneficiary information, but then allow individual beneficiaries to use vouchers to choose from among any of a number of competitive sources of information. A voucher to spend on information on the Medicare plans in my local area might well help me as much as any website maintained by the Centers for Medicare and Medicaid Services, however well executed and helpful.

Data on Medicare Choices

Ensuring that consumers are able to make wise choices among different plans is, then, a critical element of constructing an efficient market-based Medicare system. Are there data we can examine that shed light on how well Medicare choices are (or could be) made, and on ways in which they might be made better?

This is a hard question to answer for two reasons. First, it is absolutely certain that beneficiaries vary in their desire and ability to make choices. As already noted, good performance of market-like arrangements does not require that all buyers be willing or able to make good choices; only a critical mass is necessary. There is no "typical Medicare beneficiary" whose ability and tastes can be measured; some elderly recipients are poorly educated, cognitively impaired, and depressed, while others are as eager, brilliant, and decisive as they ever were (and they have more time to research their insurance options than they did before retirement). So averages are not helpful, and anecdotes are misleading; we need statistical proportions.

Second, what matters is not really the difficulty (in some general sense) of making choices, but rather how good the outcomes are in terms of each choice. "Confusion," for instance, does not really matter if it occurs in situations where almost any choice is about as good as any other. Beneficiaries may be confused by Medicare Part D precisely because the many choices are really not different from each other in ways that are material to the great bulk of the population. Outcomes are, of course, not all that matters; having to rule out lots of options that turn out to be equivalent can consume a lot of time. But getting a metric of welfare here is very hard.

This problem shows up with the early evidence on the rollout of Medicare Part D. Surveys of seniors suggest that most who signed up for it found the process easy, but a sizable minority (a quarter to a third) of those who selected it voluntarily did not rate the process highly, and about a quarter of eligibles stayed away because (among other things) they were worried about its complexity. Is that success or failure? Compared to what? Almost certainly, after the dust clears, and given the heavy subsidy to the program, the vast majority of those who ran the choice gantlet will be better off than if there were no Part D program. But that does not tell us whether the quasi-market arrangement is better than some alternative. About all we can say at this point is that the process is working, but in an imperfect way.

Some research on seniors' choices may help us understand what is (or could be) happening with the choice process. The elderly who have signed up for Part D have largely gone with two insurers, United Health Care and Humana. This pattern is not random. United (with 27 percent of the sign-ups) has a contract with AARP; a reasonable inference is that people who trust AARP to make a reasonable selection followed the association's advice. Humana, after setting low premiums, made aggressive efforts to set up informational kiosks in big-box stores and contracted with the well-regarded State Farm Insurance Company to use its agents. These could be interpreted as reasonable ways to provide information, to which customers responded in a reasonable way (Lueck and Fuhrmanns 2006).

Eleven companies, including United and Humana, signed up about 80 percent of all beneficiaries who enrolled in Part D. Part of the attraction of these companies might be that they all have well-known brand names, but this is not the whole reason behind buyers' choices. Some large insurers failed to gain substantial market share. Medicare beneficiaries demonstrated they are discriminating by *not* going with Cigna, another very large health insurer, because that company offered a high-priced product (although one that covered more drugs). The overall pattern is very far from what one would expect if choices were being made in an unthinking, random fashion.

Whether these are wise enrollee choices or not remains to be seen. The views on the rollout of Medicare Part D have been highly politicized, with both sides reciting from lists of talking points in

lieu of analysis. Democrats talk about a "confusing debacle" involv-
ing "giveaways to drug and insurance companies," while
Republicans cite high participation in the program as evidence of
success. Recent poll results provide support for both views. Nearly
two-thirds of those enrolled in the program reported they were saving money, and about the same proportion regarded the "cost" to be
reasonable (*Philadelphia Inquirer* 2006)—figures that might be read
as measures of success. They also imply, however, that about a third
of those who signed up think they are paying too much for something that does not meet their needs; and any profit-seeking firm
that found a third of customers for a new product highly dissatisfied
would think itself to be a failure.

Part D as a Voucher Plan with Private Price-Setting

While both Medicare Advantage and Part D plans have similar
informational needs, Part D plans differ from the long-term arrangement used by Medicare for choice of hospital and physician coverage in a number of ways. Most obviously, there is no public plan for
coverage of prescription drugs, much less one with a dominant market share, and thus no public plan cost to set the size of the voucher.
Rather, private plans propose premiums for a defined set of drugs to
be covered, with some flexibility in what each plan might have on
its formulary. These financial proposals help to determine the government contribution (with a little geographic adjustment). There is
still a predetermined amount from the perspective of any particular
plan, but the premium proposals help to set it.

These competitive private plans must engage in their own price
negotiations with drug companies; government price-setting is not
allowed. Some critics claim this leads to higher prices than if the
government had been a major (or the only) purchaser, although the
Congressional Budget Office assumed that average prices would be
as low under private haggling as under government procurement
(U.S. Congress, Congressional Budget Office 2004).

There is no way to determine what might have happened if a
government plan had been created that negotiated prices directly

with pharmaceutical companies. However, the strategy private plans could pursue to get a lower price—demanding that a pharmaceutical company give them a fair deal in order for their product to be included in the plan—is one that a single large public plan would have had much more difficulty following. A private insurer can leave a drug out because beneficiaries can usually find another plan that does cover it, and drug companies are willing to offer discounts to build market share. Neither of these conditions would be likely with a single public plan; even the kind of formulary bargaining that was successful for the Veterans Administration's captive audience would play less well for a politically powerful senior constituency led to expect that Medicare would pay for whatever their doctors ordered. A closer parallel would be government bargaining in Vaccines for Children (VFC), a federally funded program that provides health-care providers with free vaccines for lower-income children. The government purchases most of the vaccines used by private doctors as well as public clinics; large discounts are obtained for off-patent products, but they tend to be quite modest for patent-protected vaccines (Institute of Medicine 2003). Presumably this difference exists because, beyond exerting political pressure, the government does not really have bargaining power (in the sense of being able and willing to walk away if the price is too high), particularly when the drug's value to patients is high and the government has granted a legal monopoly to the pharmaceutical manufacturer through the patent system.

Government can do a good job when a product is supplied competitively and competing firms are willing to submit low bids in hopes of winning the contract for the whole market. But this kind of commodity-bidding probably would not cover much of the Medicare drug bill. We cannot prove that competing private plans have tightened price restraints in Part D more than the government would have done, but there are good reasons to think that any difference would not be large unless and until the government were willing to adopt a kind of jawboning approach to bargaining that would open the door for heavy-duty political lobbying, side payments, and the like. Creating a public plan that can negotiate whatever deals it can get and having it compete on a level playing field with private Part D plans might be a way to settle what is ultimately an empirical question, but one may wonder whether a public plan could ever avoid being special.

The Number of Plans in Equilibrium

The primary threat to market-like options in Medicare comes not from too many plans, but from too few. Erosion of options is certainly what happened in the late 1990s, when the Balanced Budget Act restricted growth in the dollar value of the voucher. Many private plans left numerous local markets, and no new ones entered. Yet few would call that period a golden age of Medicare policy. Somewhat surprisingly, that experience suggests that the equilibrium number of plans is quite delicately balanced and can be dramatically affected by relatively small shifts in the size of the defined contribution.

Evidence in other insurance markets suggests further that the number of competing health insurance companies affects premiums, profits, and benefits, especially for HMO options (Pauly, Hillman, Kim, and Brown 2002). Evidence also indicates that the number of insurers per market has been declining in recent years. How many separate insurance companies there are bears very little relationship to how many different plans are offered, since a single company can offer plans with many levels of coverage and different organizational structures (HMO, PPO, POS, and so forth). The main impact of number of sellers on product variety is that the number of different networks is, to some extent, related to the number of different firms; but even here, most network plans have, in recent years, had very similar networks.

In contrast to the small and shrinking number of different insurers in many markets, Medicare Part D was able to bring forth a great many plans in almost all markets. What is the relationship between the number of plans and market competition? Three influences potentially determine the equilibrium number of for-profit plans: pure administrative costs, managed-care costs, and network organization costs. To the extent that these costs are fixed per company, economies of scale will limit the number of firms in competitive markets. Of course, as suggested above, if the price is set and maintained above the competitive level, many small firms can prosper even when there are economies of scale. This may have been the case for Medicare Part D, and for Medicare HMOs in the pre–Balanced Budget Act era.

In the markets where the bulk of the population lives, important unexploited economies of scale in the supply of health insurance plans in general are not apparent. The costs to market and pay claims for indemnity insurance benefits do have a fixed component, especially in terms of information-processing costs. But those costs are generally so low relative to premiums (on the order of 5 percent) that any mid-sized plan can spread them well enough so as to make little difference in breakeven premiums. The costs to manage care (such as setting protocols and monitoring providers) are slightly more important quantitatively, but generally they are not fixed and can also be spread over many lives. The only component of costs and strategy that might have some natural monopoly properties is associated with setting up and maintaining networks. Negotiating contracts is costly, and moderate-sized markets may not be able to support a large number of differentiated networks.

If economies of scale are, indeed, small, the most immediate implication is that a relatively large number of plans would be expected to emerge. A small number, however, need not threaten to reduce competition as long as entry is open. It is the potential number of competitors, not the actual number, that matters.

Small numbers may not be of much concern for some other reasons as well. Virtually all Medicare markets can have the traditional Medicare plan, a "Blue" plan or other nonprofit, and at least one conventional investor-owned plan. The government plan serves as a constraint on any serious monopoly pricing by the private plans.

What Alternatives Make Sense?

The alternative to consumer choice in Medicare is obviously not an omniscient, benevolent government that will place each beneficiary in exactly the plan that maximizes that person's utility and minimizes the excess of payments over costs. Instead, it is almost surely the single government plan represented by the traditional Medicare program. That this plan is not a good fit for most preferences is obvious from the fact that nearly 80 percent of beneficiaries are in one of a wide variety of supplemental Medicare plans—far from taking the one-size-fits-all plan, as the great majority have opted for costly alterations.

It is not even obvious why adding more options to the government plan need make much of a difference. Suppose that initially I could choose among ten different Medicare plans. The economic model of how I should make that choice is based on search theory. Assuming it is costly to me to investigate each additional option, I decide how many to explore by comparing the benefits of checking out one more—which offers a chance of finding a better option than the one I like best among those already investigated—with the cost in time and brainwork of making that additional search. If I decide to stop searching before I check out all ten options, it follows that I will not search any further or be any more unhappy if more options are added as long as I can be sure that none of them will be superior to the first ten. And even if I do see a chance that one of the new options is better, unless the odds rise significantly or unless the variety of plans gives me better information, it will make little difference to what I do.

The literature on decision-making suggests that the real costs of additional options do not arise in a rational search model like the one just described. Instead, the best case for harm is if people are strongly affected by "regret" that they might not have gotten the best possible deal. This type of frustration surely occurs, but the evidence that it matters or is harmful is mixed. Sometimes adding choices makes it less likely that consumers will choose a particular product, and sometimes it makes it more likely (at least up to a point). The foundation here hardly seems a firm enough one on which to build a public policy of seriously restricting options. Finally, as already suggested, markets can be quick to offer consumers the service of helping them with their choices, including (if so desired) the restriction of the set of options; packaged vacations, *prix fixe* restaurant menus, and single-brand auto dealerships all suggest that this can happen, although choice restriction usually saves rather than costs money.

The final information issue to explore is strongly related to Medicare's future problems. One piece of information likely to become most valuable to beneficiaries is a plan's policy toward adoption and use of beneficial but costly new technology. On its face, conveying information to buyers about a plan's policy toward many different technologies for treating many different diseases is highly challenging. A plan can simplify this process by using cost-effectiveness analysis to make these decisions and tell consumers what its cutoff value is: "We approve all new technologies whose additional cost per quality-adjusted life year is no more than $100,000," for instance. (Such a plan would surely be lower in cost than today's Medicare, which covers technologies that are much less cost-effective.) Then consumers can choose rationally among plans, and plans can behave systematically. Even litigation might be reduced, since a plan should usually be able to prove that it followed its own announced policy, regardless of patient or physician claims about medical need.

To sum up: While Medicare beneficiaries surely do not satisfy the textbook model of fully informed buyers, they may well have enough relevant information to make the market work. The kind of information whose absence they most bemoan would help them engage in bad behavior that causes markets to be inefficient, such as adverse selection (not offset by risk adjustment) and related doctor-shopping. And the ability of real governments to make better choices for beneficiaries than they would, in the aggregate, make for themselves is far from demonstrated. With some public subsidy of information, designation of fallback or safe-harbor insurance options, a reasonable amount of minimum-quality regulation, and assistance of nongovernmental organizations, the problem of informed choice in a Medicare market can be managed.

Given this information, allowing or even encouraging options other than traditional Medicare will have benefits. If the Medicare market is unbiased, the number of private plans that will choose to enter and survive will depend in part on the diversity of preferences among beneficiaries about which types of plans they like best, as well as on any economies of scale in plan operation. If the signals are right, markets should be capable of generating close to the right number of plans in most settings. As noted earlier, a minimum of four or five sellers as a rule of thumb might be a reasonable target.

4

What Kind of Competition?

Over the years, several different concepts or models of competition in health insurance markets have been advocated. While Medicare has not been the first target of this advocacy, supporters generally suppose the program can benefit from competition in some way. How could health care markets be structured to promote robust competition?

The earliest attempt to discuss texture, relevance, and persuasiveness of competitive markets in health care and insurance was Alain Enthoven's notion of "managed competition" (1974). While the idea was more general than is customarily realized, Enthoven in his own writing strongly identified managed competition with a choice among competing managed-care insurance plans, and expected that the plan regarded best would be a closed-panel,[1] fully integrated insurance and delivery management system with minimal cost-sharing, like the Kaiser Permanente health plans.

The next notion of an attractive competitive model was, in many ways, a reaction to the HMO model. Advanced most strongly by the National Center for Policy Analysis in Dallas (Serafini 2004), it proposed offering tax incentives to consumers to choose high-deductible health plans, coupled with tax-shielded health or medical savings accounts. While managed care envisioned resource-allocation choices being made by the management of a health plan at risk for high cost, this catastrophic health plan/health savings account approach—rechristened consumer-directed health care—put the patient at financial risk to generate incentives to contain costs, helped by copious amounts of information to be made available on the Internet.

The third and most recent model of competition is the "value-based competition" advocated by Michael Porter and Elizabeth Teisberg (2006). This approach supposes that providers of medical care will be organized to provide identifiable "care cycle" packages for different medical conditions (such as diabetes or heart disease). Information on the outcomes and prices of similar packages offered by different suppliers will permit consumers who have insurance with some cost-sharing to select a bundled care package that offers the greatest value for the money.

There has been considerable debate among the advocates of these three forms of competition, as well as with those opposed to competition in any form (both for private insurance markets and for publicly subsidized populations like those on Medicare), about which approach is best. The voucher arrangement I have described for Medicare, however, makes such a mutually exclusive framing of this question unnecessary. In particular, in the reasonably large Medicare markets that prevail nationwide, consumers might select any of the three types of insurance and care delivery, depending on how they value the tradeoffs inherent in each option. They might use their vouchers to cover all or part of the cost of competing managed-care plans, of competing high-deductible health plans with spending accounts (with or without Porter-Teisberg care-cycle–based competition), or of bundled and à la carte medical-care delivery systems.

The reason to follow this route rather than anoint one or the other model as the best is that each model has pluses and minuses, which different people probably will value in different ways. One approach may eventually come to dominate, if indeed it is superior; but that kind of outcome should come from competitive markets, rather than being imposed on them a priori.

The main tradeoff is between the care coordination advantages of bundling (maximized in the fully integrated HMO, present to some extent in care cycles) and the greater consumer information and foresight required when the beneficiary initially selects the plan, versus the lower information demands and greater flexibility of the consumer-directed health plan. I have already commented on the informational needs in choosing among the largely HMO-type

Medicare Advantage plans. Because a person who chooses a managed-care plan will be bound by its rules for all medical conditions, the informational burden is obviously quite heavy; but the care can be fully integrated across the variety of simultaneous medical conditions which typically afflict the elderly. The Porter-Teisberg model works best if a person suffers from only one independent and easily definable medical condition at a time, and it assumes that tamper-proof information on final outcomes (not information from process measures, as provided at present in virtually all report cards) can be generated. If those assumptions could turn into reality, competition would work better; but with errors necessarily occurring in identification of conditions and in measurement of outcomes, there are bound to be some mistakes overall. Finally, while the do-it-yourself care management embodied in consumer-directed care offers the prospect of lower costs on average, it is at the expense of greater exposure to negative effects of financial risk and consumer mistakes.

As Porter and Teisberg note, improvement in the functioning of markets should come spontaneously out of competitive urges present in such markets, unless government or private conspiracy gets in the way. They argue, in fact, that American medical markets are already well on the way toward their value-based model. The tax-financed subsidy inherent in Medicare adds a complication to this optimistic view, since the subsidy puts government initially in the driver's seat. Advocates of Medicare Advantage plans then challenge government to abdicate control over medical benefits and prices. Porter and Teisberg do advocate that government should help their model along by redesigning the traditional Medicare plan with more bundling (a proposition that Medicare analysts have tussled with for years without finding the right and politically accepted balance).

The voucher approach would not necessarily require the public insurance plan to take the lead, either in high deductibles or bundled payment, if indeed it competed on a level playing field; some set of private plans could just as well pioneer this approach with less political fallout. The best policy for government might be to make sure that all of these options are initially made available, and then get out of the way.

The Simple Voucher Model and Real-World Complexities

My argument so far is that a simple voucher approach, supplemented by enforced quality standards, public funding for information, and risk adjustment, is in theory consistent with a market-like arrangement, with some highly desirable properties even in the short-run static setting. I have already suggested that actual Medicare arrangements appear to come fairly close to this simple model. But are there more complex features in the actual program design that weaken the link between theory and current feasible practice?

There are two key elements in any voucher program: how the voucher amounts are determined, and how suppliers can structure their offerings around the voucher. As already noted, historically the size of the private-plan voucher was linked to the cost of the traditional Medicare program. It is this link that leads to terminological confusion: All Medicare plans were required to provide at least the benefit that the traditional plan furnished (so in this sense there was a "defined benefit," although that definition was somewhat elastic and changeable over time), and then the cost of this plan determined the dollar amount of the voucher for private plans (so in this sense set up the value of a defined contribution). Medicare has traditionally been a hybrid between defined (health) benefit and defined contribution. From an economic viewpoint the contribution was more fundamental than the benefit, since the benefit might fail to be delivered if the funding were insufficient. But that kind of hybrid is precisely the desirable arrangement I have been describing: a risk-adjusted voucher for qualified plans.

Up to this point, I have treated the traditional Medicare plan as just one among a number of competing plans, possibly special in terms of setting the benchmark but not otherwise differing from other options. This approach ignores the political history of traditional Medicare and its place in the Medicare system.

While there may be little reason in bloodless policy analysis to worry about the effect of market arrangements in Medicare, emotions such as pride, nostalgia, or fear may be involved. Medicare has been, as noted, one of the most popular government programs and, despite being forty years old, remains the youngest grandchild of the New Deal still alive in Washington. Many support it for that political and philosophical reason and are fiercely protective of this memorial. While not all emotions can bear further analysis, it probably is useful to examine the fear of upsetting the political bargain that is associated with any program to reduce the large market share of the traditional public Medicare plan.

One version of this fear is that the middle class as a whole will cease to support Medicare if they do not see it as a deal sufficiently attractive to themselves to justify a large transfer payment to those with lower lifetime earnings who (at least nominally) get the same insurance benefit. Whether such transfers actually occur has been challenged by some researchers who note the longer lives and more costly use of services by higher-income beneficiaries (McClellan and Skinner 1997). Of course, if some private alternative can deliver even more to all, this apprehension should not matter. But a more visceral fear is that, if one support is weakened, the whole house of cards may come tumbling down. The fact that Medicaid, an explicitly aggressive means-tested program, has survived and even expanded over time could be interpreted as a piece of historical counterevidence.

The best kind of voucher-based competition treats all insurers meeting standards for quality in a neutral way; given the value of the voucher, no additional public intervention is required once the rules are set up. The choice of the benchmark value of the voucher, in contrast, is at base fundamentally political. Observations on cost incurred among competing plans should serve well in the short run as a way of selecting this value. In the longer term, democratic political choice must necessarily be the way values will be set.

5

Painful but Unavoidable Adjustment

Given the possible advantages of market competition in Medicare, why then (as I asked earlier) is the traditional plan so generally popular? A large part of the reason stems from the historical ability of the financing system to deliver an intrinsically attractive product at a low cost to beneficiaries and at a cost to taxpayers that is both moderate and hidden.

The reason for Medicare's attractiveness to seniors is not hard to find: Their premiums amounted to only 10 percent of the cost of the benefit before the advent of Part D and only about 12 percent afterward. This represents an enormous subsidy to seniors, and virtually any product, no matter how imperfect, would be attractive at this kind of discount.

Why Medicare is attractive to the population at large is more subtle and more important. Suffice it to say that as long as the annual growth in the number of persons going on Medicare was moderate relative to the growth in the number of workers and taxpayers paying for Medicare, it was easy to promise benefits displaying good value relative to expected taxes. This was certainly true in the early days of Medicare, when there were few beneficiaries and many contributors, and the anticipated net benefit has remained positive (though shrinking) over time.

But the combination of the baby boom retirement with the baby bust in birthrates has put the demographic perpetual-motion machine into reverse. All one can see to the infinite horizon is an expanding gap between projected Medicare costs and revenues generated by Medicare taxes. The trustees forecast that, even assuming that future spending growth will taper off and the tax base will continue to grow, tax rates needed to fund spending will double or triple from current levels within the next twenty to forty years.[1] While I will give more of the quantitative details below, the unequivocal message is clear: Medicare's current promised coverage, if extended to the medical services likely to be available in coming years, implies a high tax rate that plausibly and prudently cannot be sustained.

What the change will (or should) be is one key question, which I will also address in detail. But at this point the main conclusion is that Medicare benefits in the future are going to have to be more limited than those implied by today's coverage for at least a large fraction of the beneficiary population. Faced with the necessity for limits, the program can choose one of two routes. It can determine, in some fashion or other, what limits on the traditional Medicare benefit will be necessary, and uniformly confront beneficiaries with those limits. Or it can limit its contribution to spending, but permit beneficiaries to choose in a market of options what insurance coverage they now prefer in the face of this limit. I argue that, both in terms of what is right and what makes political sense, the latter approach is preferable. That is, given the dramatic shift in Medicare's prospects, the popularity of the dominant public plan is sure to wane. Given that they may have to make or be subject to cutbacks, people will want the ability to decide how that is to be accomplished, and their choices will require market-based arrangements.

Alternative Program Solutions

If government cannot be expected to finance new technology for Medicare in the future at the same rate as in the past, what alternatives are available for the program? As may be expected, the solutions that sound relatively painless are also relatively useless, although they may help a little for awhile; whereas the solutions that may work may seem nearly unthinkable. Here I discuss three possible solutions: means-tested premiums, means-tested benefits, and limited-growth vouchers. The last of these is most consistent with the market-based approach I have been discussing.

Means-Tested Premiums. Perhaps the most obvious way to reduce the prospective and unaffordable burden on future taxpayers and lower-income beneficiaries is to raise the premium for the standard Medicare package that is charged to higher-income retirees. A very small step in this direction was included in the 2003 Medicare Modernization Act (MMA), but the higher premiums only apply to Part B and to people with near or above six-figure incomes. Because the proportion of people at all ages who are so rich is relatively low and drops even more when a population retires, the financial benefit of this step will be small. Moreover, further increasing the share of the premium charged to this income group may drive the healthier and richer to forgo Medicare Part B. Of course, if enrollment in all the parts of Medicare were made mandatory, as it is for Part A, this might be less of a problem, but then individuals might drop Medicare entirely (which is possible, but only if those people also relinquish their Social Security benefits). The only way to find a large enough base among seniors to support any serious contribution to Medicare's fiscal problem is to base premiums on wealth (including the value of owned housing) as well as explicit cash income, but even doing this might not be enough to keep the high-income population in Medicare.

Inducing higher-income beneficiaries to drop out would represent an alteration of Medicare's traditional role of insurer for all of the over–sixty-five population. Some people see adverse social and political consequences of such segmentation, as this population would presumably be less supportive of the program. Were it possible to keep the group together, we would not be contemplating this step. At least one advantage to the departure of the well-off would be that the government would no longer have to pay for their health benefits. After all, once they retire, even well-off beneficiaries, for the most part, no longer pay their own way (even though they might have paid much more than their cost over their lifetimes). Since higher-income people tend to cost Medicare more than others (at least from a lifetime perspective), shedding them might be less adverse than might be thought. Having a means-tested program affordable for taxpayers in general might be more desirable than having all seniors backing a fiscally unsustainable pooled program.

Means-Tested Benefits. While means-testing premiums will help Medicare's finances, the effect would surely be modest and probably temporary. This approach, unfortunately, would do nothing to address the escalating cost of the benefit package, which is the ultimate and major cause of the fiscal meltdown. A second strategy, then, might be to means-tests benefits, providing less coverage as income rises. There is precedent for this in the MMA as well: Medicare Part D offers much more generous coverage to lower-income seniors than to those at average and higher incomes, who are presented with a policy metaphorically described as a donut, with a major hole in coverage.

Let us assume that any reductions in coverage, either in terms of higher cost-sharing or limits on coverage for some services, would be accompanied by permission to higher-income people to select voluntarily supplemental private coverage for what the traditional plans now begin to exclude. There are surely possibilities for modest increases in deductibles (especially the Part B deductible) for high-income seniors, and perhaps for bumping up the parts B and D copayments a little. These changes might even reduce total spending a little if they are not wholly offset by supplementary coverage (though past Medigap experience is not especially encouraging). Like the first strategy, this approach also suffers from small numbers and dropout possibilities; the beneficiary presumably sticks with Part B by comparing the premium with the expected over-average benefit, and the value of this mix can be made negative almost as easily by cutting benefits as by raising premiums.

An alternative that I proposed earlier, perhaps less subject to this problem, involves focusing more directly on the source of rising cost per person: the beneficial but expensive new medical technology that will almost certainly be added over time, even with constant nominal coverage (Pauly 2004). This solution is aimed not so much at cutting the level of cost but rather at cutting its rate of growth, which is the source of the problem. Medicare's promise to better-off beneficiaries would be limited to paying in the future for today's new technology—that is, for today's level of real benefits. (This would probably require limiting coverage for some new technologies and providing no coverage for others.) A beneficiary who feels that any new technology above this level is not worth its additional cost will be able to exclude it from coverage. With the remaining package perhaps more highly valued as a result, the beneficiary may continue to pay premiums and accept coverage, especially if the limit applies to all parts of Medicare, not just to Part B (or parts B and D).

Limited-Growth Vouchers. Rather than tampering either with premiums for existing coverage or limits to current benefits, however, probably the best way to contain spending for higher-income beneficiaries and yet still retain Medicare as an option for them is through a voucher approach. Unless the beneficiary premium increases dramatically or the person's risk becomes very small, there will be a difference between the value of the voucher (and the benefits it buys) and the premium that will prompt virtually all to remain in Medicare in some fashion. Because the voucher can be used for the kind of coverage most valuable to the beneficiary, it will be even more reasonable to continue to pay a modest premium for a flexible voucher of much greater value. Moreover, rather than trying to make a distinction between new technology and old technology, providing a voucher allows the beneficiary to decide what old technology to keep, what new technology to add, what new technology to limit, and what old technology to discard in favor of the new technology. In short, the best way (at least in theory) to preserve Medicare as an attractive option for the great majority of beneficiaries and yet limit government-financed payment growth is to move toward a voucher with a limited growth rate, and then allow beneficiaries to use their vouchers among a variety of plans with fairly light restrictions on minimum levels of coverage.

What do we know about how such "semimarket" plans might work for Medicare beneficiaries, compared to traditional Medicare alone, and what needs to be done in the future?

6

Markets Without Magic

Much of the political enthusiasm for market-based reforms in Medicare is based on a wish for magical cost-cutting powers. Given the high present costs for the traditional plan, its rapid rate of growth (8 percent in 2004), and its dire future financial situation, can we harness the efficiency of private markets to contain costs? The empirical evidence so far indicates that the answer to this question is probably not, at least not without further big changes.

To achieve low or slower-growing total costs in an insurance plan, one must either affect prices or quantities. The traditional Medicare plan probably has had the power to lower or slow the growth of unit prices and fees more than its modestly sized, private managed-care competitors. However, private integrated, capitated plans potentially have greater ability to lower the quantity of services, largely on the inpatient side, using both direct incentives and better-designed substitutes of less costly items (like drugs) for more costly ones (like inpatient care).

Early evidence comparing the total cost of private Medicare HMOs with the public plan, using more or less similar prices, found that the private plans appeared to attract lower risks but did not lower the government's cost, though they might have lowered total resource costs if HMO enrollees paid less for their health care than equivalent beneficiaries in traditional Medicare (Brown et al. 1993). As I suggested would occur when the 1997 Balanced Budget Act was about to be passed and many commentators were predicting strong advantages for private plans from its provisions, what actually happened was that private plans could not match the traditional plan's ability to control provider reimbursement growth to a below-trend target (Pauly 1996). The traditional plan could (and did) lower the annual update in payments to providers, but the private plans could not, and so lost market share while exiting the marketplace in relatively large numbers. This advantage for the traditional Medicare plan, however, depended on its ability to use its large market share to extract discounts from providers who were reluctant, but nevertheless unwilling to forgo traditional Medicare entirely. That ability was obviously limited; providers would not lower prices indefinitely. It was also dependent on a large market share that would (and perhaps should) erode over time.

For Medicare Part D, the Congressional Budget Office estimated that competing private plans would be as effective as a single government plan in lowering prices paid to drug companies (U.S. Congress, Congressional Budget Office 2004), but that was because of private plans' ability to exclude certain items from coverage, an option that was not available previously for private managed-care coverage. In all cases, however, the early differences in cost or cost growth have been quite small; there has as yet been no sign of cost-containment magic, though the initial levels of cost and premiums look good relative to the Medicare actuary's estimates made before the start of Part D. How robust this will be over time only time itself can tell.

What is most puzzling in the traditional coverage plans, and what remains to be established in the case of Part D, is the profitability and entry or exit of private plans as a function of the size of the implicit voucher. For the traditional coverage, the experience of the Balanced Budget Act after 1997 and Medicare Advantage suggests close to a knife-edge behavior. Private plans can thrive with the voucher at a certain size, but a relatively modest cut in the value (or the rate of growth in value) of the voucher causes them to lose money in competition with the public plan and, consequently, to exit in droves. An equally modest upward bump in the size of the private plan contribution has caused the enrollment proportion in Medicare Advantage plans to surge from 12 percent to almost 20 percent from 2000 to 2007.

We do not yet know the story for Part D because there is (so far) no government-managed alternative to private plans for drug benefits. A very large number of drug-only private plans entered in response to Part D, and an addition to the size of the voucher helped full-coverage private plans with drug benefits. The public subsidy in Part D was not specified explicitly, nor was it tied to the cost in a public plan. Rather, the specifications of coverage were set, and firms were free to come in with lower premiums—and many did. We have no evidence that private plans have differed from the public plan in terms of the cost growth rate. Even in the happy years, private Medicare HMOs apparently tracked the traditional plan, with no evidence of greater undercutting over time.

How a Cost-Contained Medicare Program Might Work

As already noted, the key ingredient in determining both government cost and private plan participation in market-based Medicare is the level of the government payment—the defined contribution or dollar value of the voucher. Except for the new Part D, all previous variants of private plans in Medicare—the HMO option, Medicare Plus Choice, and Medicare Advantage—have determined this amount by linking it to the risk-adjusted cost of the traditional plan at current benefit levels. Three other broad classes of mechanisms for determining this amount should be considered: a full-blown competitive bidding arrangement, a predetermined growth-rate model, and a political-administrative expenditure-setting model. How might each of these mechanisms work, and does it matter which is used?

The latter question is actually the easier to deal with. For almost all intents and purposes, only the dollar amount of Medicare payment, not the method by which it is determined, will matter. The argument is simple: Suppose in some fashion or other, Medicare decides it will pay X number of dollars toward my insurance coverage, regardless of which plan I select. This amount will be adjusted by characteristics that predict my expense, including, obviously, some measures of my health status, but perhaps also my geographic location, income, wealth, or educational level, and whether I live in a nursing home or in my own home in the broader community.

Once my payment level is given, both the public plans (differing from today's traditional Medicare) and private plans must determine what coverage they can offer me at whatever additional net premium they might charge. Competition among providers of insurance may be expected to bid insurer profits down to the minimum competitive level (at least in the long run), so that the cost of my benefits, given my premium, is determined. In effect, competition makes sure that any premium I pay, plus the value of my voucher turned over to the insurer I choose, will buy me the maximum dollar value of benefits it is possible to offer. The precise mix or configuration of benefits of equal actuarial value may vary across plans, and competition also means that plans will try to find combinations that match my preferences, and/or that I find attractive.

This has an important implication. Setting a higher voucher level is undesirable only to the extent that the additional benefits that will be furnished are worth less than their additional cost. Since the "social worth" of Medicare benefits is necessarily imprecise and intrinsically political, a judgment on a particular method for setting the payment level is valid only in the context of collective choice; there is no technical inefficiency necessarily associated with a higher cost that pays for benefits that are worth it.

To be precise, suppose we set the voucher at the cost of the traditional Medicare plan, and suppose (for the sake of argument) that this plan is inefficient in the sense that benefits of equal value could feasibly be produced at lower cost. In ideal competitive equilibrium, no informed beneficiary will be in the traditional plan, and the high realized budgetary cost will be excessive only if the original nominal Medicare benefits were judged fully adequate; in the real world, we should be able to get close to an outcome in which payments transform into real benefits (or premium refunds) rather than substantial excess profits. (There could be problems in rural areas where it is harder for traditional managed-care plans to compete, but Medicare fee-for-service plans should be able to provide some competition.) The rhetoric about linking Medicare payment to a potentially inefficient, high-cost public bureaucracy, even if true, overstates the kind of inefficiency that will result; the final outcome will not be one with very inefficient production, but rather one with excessively generous benefits efficiently produced.

Enormous effort has gone into designing an alternative way of setting the voucher that would involve a kind of competitive bidding process to provide the nominal package of benefits (Dowd, Coulam, and Feldman 2000). The primary rationale is to break the link between public spending and the cost of the traditional Medicare program, which might be inflated by inefficiency. Rather than simply set a lower payment rate and challenge private plans to deliver Medicare's required benefits for that level of funding, the idea is that the lowest bid will represent both the minimum cost that might be expected and identification of a plan able and willing to deliver standard benefits for that amount of money.

Despite substantial and imaginative design work on such a system, the government has not been able to mount any genuine demonstrations of full competitive bidding models for all parts of Medicare. Attempts to do so get bogged down in red tape, in the government's desire to guarantee cost savings, and in political objections from the targeted local area, concerned that it will be forced to be low-cost when no one else is. Based on the earlier analysis, this fear is well-founded, since private plans will deliver less if their revenues are lowered.

A more modest bidding approach has, as noted, been implemented for Part D. With no government program, the benchmark payment level must be linked to something else. In the case of Part D, plans still bid, and their bids relative to the benchmark effectively set the premiums they will charge. The largest part of the benchmark payment depends on the nationwide weighted-average bid (adjusted for reinsurance subsidies) for a standardized package of benefits. Both ex ante risk adjustment and forecasted ex post reinsurance subsidies (effectively an additional plan-specific risk adjustment that depends on the coverage offered as well as "objective" risk) set the benchmark. While the process is somewhat complex, in the end the plan chooses the kind of coverage it will offer; the more generous the coverage and the more permissive its policies, the higher the premium it will charge in the market. Thus, in a rough and ready (though not very transparent) fashion, beneficiaries can choose between low-premium plans that provide somewhat less generous monetary values of benefits, and high-premium plans with higher expected benefits.

A third strategy is to choose a payment level linked in some way to current levels of spending, but then establish a rule for the long-run growth of spending. Given the importance of spending increases, the growth formula would become much more important in determining the voucher amount than the initial level. An approach of this type has been implemented for physician payment in Medicare, with growth for that subset of spending required to fall on a sustainable growth path linked to growth in the GDP.

The main analytic problem with such a rules-based approach is obvious: There is no reason to expect that a target linked, ultimately, to what the nation's tax system can easily afford (or is willing to make available) will track well the medical technology that is just worth what it costs. Given current knowledge, however, trying to find the best solution to this complex planning problem is probably counsel of despair. We do not even know the long-run average rate of growth consistent with efficient development and application of new technology (assuming it is lower than what we currently experience). More to the point, I know of no method, even a speculative one, that would establish how much of each year's potential increase in spending would represent technology that is worth what it costs. In light of this ignorance, setting the voucher's growth at some level that is politically and economically sustainable might actually be a reasonable place to start.

The closest we have come to gaining experience with this strategy has been the "sustainable growth rate" for physician payment under Medicare Part B. In that case, however, Medicare's instrument was the unit price, whereas the target was total expenses (price times quantity). Thus, awkward procedures were needed for readjusting prices depending on what happened to quantity. In the case of a voucher for premiums, this issue would not arise.

The final strategy (which could be thought of as a modification of the previous one) is simply to set a politically chosen growth rate and to monitor in some fashion the dimensions of quality that matter from a social perspective: the cost-effectiveness of care, the extent of financial protection, and consumer outcomes and satisfaction. Should these indicators fall "too much," that would be a sign that the constraints on growth are cutting too deeply. Determination of how much is too much, however, would probably also have to be a political process, although research could well be brought to bear on this question. Symmetry would suggest that an increase in quality would signify too high a level of payment, although this may be a more difficult political argument to make.

How the Market Will Make Cuts

The main point, then, is that even with a crude (though by definition politically acceptable) budgeting process to set the size of the payment for beneficiaries' health and the associated tax levels, market-type arrangements will make the best of the situation. Suppose that the voucher amount for Medicare coverage for non-poor beneficiaries is set at a certain level and set to grow at a rate lower than the growth rate of spending that would otherwise occur in Medicare and in the private sector. (This obviously requires suspending disbelief about the absence of political manipulation. That can never be prevented entirely, but could be reduced if government had to choose a rate of growth well in advance—if there were longer-term rules rather than shorter-term discretion.) Suppose also that costly but beneficial new technology continues to be put on the market regardless of the size of the voucher. In theory, all of the politics is supposed to be embodied in (and encapsulated by) the process that sets the payment level. Then individual Medicare plans would have to choose either to raise the premium charged to the individual to cover the new technology or to put in place some mechanisms to affect the management of care. Probably they would do some of both, with different plans adopting different mixes.

In principle, data on the cost-effectiveness of various services rendered at various levels to people with various medical conditions could be used to develop protocols, differing depending on the target value for the cost-effectiveness ratio. A plan using a higher target value would have higher total premium growth, and therefore growth in the premium the person must pay, but it would also have better access to new technology. People could choose what they liked.

The other strategy would be for each plan to announce its increase in premiums, what new services are to be provided, and which ones are not. This approach is logically the same as the first if cost-effectiveness is used to select the set; it may seem more natural to consumers, but it also will be harder to understand and use because of the high volume of information and the need for the consumer to guess what illness will occur, as well as what benefit each type of treatment (included or excluded) might provide.

It may well be that, faced with the expectation of lower Medicare payments (and therefore higher premiums if a new technology is covered, or high out-of-pocket payments if it is not), suppliers of new technology will change their pricing and product-introduction decisions. Most fundamentally, a new technology with a high cost-effectiveness ratio for all patients might never be introduced, thus avoiding the need for explicit rationing. The problem is that virtually every new technology will be appropriately cost-effective for some patients, and yet, once it is available, insurance will be forced to pay for it for people for whom it is not as cost-effective.

It is also possible that higher cost-sharing (but with some coverage) would be applied to new technologies, thus inducing insurers to make decisions on use that would filter out low-benefit–high-cost combinations. And any cost offsets resulting from the use of new technologies (such as lowered hospital costs) should be taken into account.

Developing a system to allow beneficiaries to make choices among plans adopting various methods of limiting costly technology is surely a challenge, but it is one that must be addressed. The alternative of a uniform government decision is simpler, but less attractive. Arrangements which permit choice of rationing method should be planned and (to the extent possible) tested now.

Conclusion

A storm is clearly brewing over Medicare's future, and coping with it will require beneficiary access to more choices than can be furnished by the single, dominant, government insurance plan that is traditional Medicare. Yet, paradoxically, that dominance makes it hard for the alternatives to become sufficiently established when they are needed. As already noted, it means that private plans, unable to invoke sufficient cost-controls, will have a hard time surviving, even in a neutral setting.

The commonsense strategy for someone who believes that choice needs to be created in advance is one of planned and temporary unbalancing. Given the powerful role of inertia in insurance choice and the high brand recognition for traditional Medicare, one should be honest and say that some help for new entrants may be needed. One approach might be a temporary subsidy for the private plans covering the traditional Medicare benefits. It should be matched with creation of a publicly managed drug coverage option, again placed in a neutral setting.

Disciples of the public program and believers in neutral markets (and people who are skeptical about the possibility of a temporary public subsidy) will be concerned about these transitions. This "luring of customers from Medicare" will and should be a source of bipartisan worry. And yet creating a long-term strategy with a predictable and precommitted policy toward public and private programs is necessary if private firms are to be willing to do business with the government, and beneficiaries who choose private plans are to have assurance that they will not be left stranded as victims of mercurial government policies. Mutual ideological disarmament—accepting the potential coexistence of both public and private plans in equilibrium—is difficult but essential.

With the kind of competition we know we have, it is considerable consolation that the bulk of any subsidies will ultimately benefit those beneficiaries who choose the new programs. The fears of "profiteering" (assuming that term could be defined and its existence could be detected) should be able to be allayed. Although private plans are not always explicitly ordered by government to do anything for their payments (other than provide the basic Medicare coverage), we know that they volunteer to add benefits and cut consumer costs when they compete. Private-plan decisions to enter or leave this market do seem very responsive to movements in the size of the voucher payment. Perhaps some modest additional down payment to first movers among private plans would be a small price to pay for construction of what effectively would be a Medicare safety net to protect against unilateral consternation when the inevitable meltdown of the traditional plan occurs. Under neutral arrangements, the public plan also will be faced with the need to balance its budget, given revenues from the voucher and any beneficiary premiums; discipline will have to be enforced if it runs a deficit. That will also be a challenge, but not an insurmountable one.

To those who think that the day of neutral arrangements will never come, permission for (much less subsidy of) private plans does not make much sense. If we assumed that the traditional plan could go on forever as we know it today, they would be right—but I believe the evidence that the premise is false is overwhelming. Things simply cannot go on as they are for the traditional Medicare plan. The evidence of inevitability needs to be made more salient. The primary problem is that the estimates of Medicare financial liability are so overwhelming that they produce inaction born of despair.

The reason for sustaining and creating competition in Medicare is not necessarily to save money well into the future; compared to a single public plan, competition will not necessarily save money for the program, since the government can always pay less and extract more from providers. What competition will do, even in the short run, is save money for beneficiaries and improve the quality of health care. What it must do in the long run is save Medicare.

Notes

Introduction

1. Because traditional Medicare requires substantial out-of-pocket expenditures (such as deductibles and coinsurance), many beneficiaries also have supplemental coverage. This may be purchased as private Medigap insurance, supplied through retiree health insurance or, for low-income individuals, provided through Medicaid.

Chapter 1: A Voucher by Any Other Name

1. High-deductible plans, if chosen by very low-income people, might be a counterexample, but so far no such plans have been offered.

2. See page 3.

3. A National Academy of Social Insurance study (King and Schlesinger 2003) offers a skeptic's approach to market-based Medicare.

Chapter 2: What Can Go Right, and What Can Go Wrong?

1. For further discussion of Medicare's use of risk adjustment, see Kominski 2007.

2. A similar point has been made by Lien, Ma, and McGuire (2004).

3. For example, suppose that a fifth of an insurer's customers will leave if its price is set 2 percent higher than its competitors' (for instance, an additional $200 per year). Then its markup over its (marginal) cost cannot be greater than 10 percent of its cost or (in the case of a Medicare HMO where marginal administrative costs are about 15 percent of premiums), only about 1.5 percent of the total premium.

Chapter 3: How Many Plans?

1. For evidence on the effect of bidding in health insurance markets, see Vistnes, Cooper, and Vistnes 2001.

2. There is a kind of myopia here that affects individuals' views about the optimal number of plan offerings. From a purely personal perspective, I only need to be offered the one plan that I like the best. I would staunchly advocate a single-plan, single-player approach that offered my favorite plan. Offering other, less attractive plans provides me no additional benefit, and having more choices increases my search costs. But individuals' tastes differ, so a system that offers only one plan (or very few plans) forces some people to enroll in plans they would not otherwise accept. Having multiple plans (beyond the four or so needed to control market power) will seem like a waste to most people, even though greater choice is likely to increase welfare for others in the group. If most people found plans they liked with a limited choice, they would loudly criticize the proliferation of additional plans, even though those other plans might be of great benefit to the dissatisfied minority. Here, even more than usual, expressions of general opinion are a poor guide to good public policy.

3. An example is the Federal Employees Health Benefit Program, which requires detailed information from participating plans to be distributed to federal workers and retirees, and which has also created a purely private market for comparative information on health plan choices. Such comparative information has been available from private sources for almost three decades. See Francis 2007.

Chapter 4: What Kind of Competition?

1. A closed-panel health plan contracts with physicians on an exclusive basis for services and does not allow those physicians to see patients for another health plan.

Chapter 5: Painful but Unavoidable Adjustment

1. Part A spending is estimated to be 3.1 percent of taxable payroll in 2007—only slightly higher than the 2.9 percent payroll tax rate that funds that portion of Medicare. By 2030, Part A spending will exceed 5.9 percent of payroll, or more than double the current payroll tax; by 2050, spending will exceed 8.7 percent of payroll, or more than triple the current payroll tax. See U.S. Social Security Administration, Social Security and Medicare Boards of Trustees 2007.

References

Boards of Trustees of the Federal Hospital Insurance and Federal Supplementary Medical Insurance Trust Funds. 2004. *Annual Report of the Boards of Trustees of the Federal Hospital Insurance and Federal Supplementary Medical Insurance Trust Funds.* Washington, D.C.: Government Printing Office.

Bresnahan, T., and P. Reiss. 1991. Entry and Competition in Concentrated Markets. *Journal of Political Economy* 99 (5): 977–1009.

Brown, S. Randall, Dolores G. Clement, Jerrold W. Hill, Sheldon M. Retchin, and Jeannette W. Bergeron. 1993. Do Health Maintenance Organizations Work for Medicare? *HCFA Review* 15 (1): 7–24.

Dowd, Brian, R. Coulam, and R. Feldman. 2000. A Tale of Four Cities: Medicare Reform and Competitive Pricing. *Health Affairs* 19 (5): 9–29.

Enthoven, Alain. 1974. *Health Plan.* New York: Addison Wesley.

Francis, Walton. 2007. *Checkbook's 2008 Guide to Health Plans for Federal Employees.* Washington, D.C.: Center for the Study of Services.

Gold, Marsha. 2005. Private Plans in Medicare: Another Look. *Health Affairs* 24 (5): 1302–10.

Institute of Medicine. 2003. *Financing Vaccines in the 21st Century: Assuring Access and Availability.* Washington, D.C.: National Academies Press.

King, Kathleen M., and Mark Schlesinger, eds. 2003. *The Role of Private Health Plans in Medicare: Lessons from the Past, Looking to the Future. Final Report of the Study Panel on Medicare and Markets.* Washington, D.C.: National Academy of Social Insurance, November.

Kominski, Gerald F. 2007. Medicare's Use of Risk Adjustment. National Health Policy Forum background paper. August 21. http://www.nhpf. org/pdfs_bp/BP_RiskAdjustMedicare_08-21-07.pdf (accessed September 19, 2007).

Lien, Hsien-Ming, Ching-To Albert Ma, and Thomas G. McGuire. 2004. Provider-Client Interactions and Quantity of Health Care Use. *Journal of Health Economics* 23 (6): 1261–83 .

Lueck, S., and V. Fuhrmanns. 2006. Enrollment Gains in New Drug Plans Tied to Marketing. *Wall Street Journal.* April 30, A3.

Lueck, S., and J. Zhang. 2006. Personal Health (A Special Report)—Give Us Your Sick. . . . Thanks to a Shift in Medicare Policies, Insurers are Seeking Out Those They Once Avoided. *Wall Street Journal.* October 21, R5.

Madrian, Bridgette, and Dennis Shea. 2001. The Power of Suggestion: Inertia in 401(k) Participation and Savings Behavior. *Quarterly Journal of Economics* 116 (4): 1149–87.

McClellan, Mark, and Jon Skinner. 1997. The Incidence of Medicare. NBER Working Paper No. 6013. Cambridge, Mass.: National Bureau of Economic Research, April.

Medicare Payment Advisory Commission (MedPAC). 2006. *Report to the Congress: Increasing the Value of Medicare,* June. http://www.medpac.gov/documents/Jun06_EntireReport.pdf (accessed June 14, 2007).

Pauly, M. V. 1996. Will Medicare Reforms Increase Managed Care Enrollment? *Health Affairs* 15 (3): 182–91.

———. 2004. Means-Testing in Medicare. *Health Affairs* Web Exclusive. December 8, 546–57. http://content.healthaffairs.org/cgi/reprint/hlthaff.w4.546v1 (accessed March 29, 2007).

Pauly, M. V., A. Hillman, Myoung Kim, and Darryl Brown. 2002. Competitive Behavior in the HMO Marketplace. *Health Affairs* 21 (1): 194–202.

Philadelphia Inquirer. 2006. Medicare Part D: Prescription Plan Helps, But Tweaks Are Needed. Editorial. April 30, D6.

Porter, Michael, and Elizabeth Teisberg. 2006. *Redefining Health Care: Creating Value-Based Competition and Results.* Cambridge, Mass.: Harvard Business School Press.

Serafini, Marilyn Werber. 2004. Health Care: The Father of HSAs. *National Journal* 36 (6): 396–97.

Thaler, Richard, and Cass Sunstein. 2003. Libertarian Paternalism. *American Economic Review, Papers and Proceedings* 93 (2): 175–79.

U.S. Congress. Congressional Budget Office. 2004. Douglas Holtz-Eakin (director) to William H. Frist (U.S. Senate majority leader). January 23. http://www.cbo.gov/ftpdocs/49xx/doc4986/FristLetter.pdf (accessed January 17, 2008).

U.S. Social Security Administration. Social Security and Medicare Boards of Trustees. 2007. *Status of the Social Security and Medicare Programs: A Summary of the 2007 Annual Reports.* http://www.ssa.gov/OACT/TRSUM/trsummary.html (accessed October 25, 2007).

Vistnes, Jessica P., Phillip F. Cooper, and Gregory S. Vistnes. 2001. Employer Contribution Methods and Health Insurance Premiums: Does

Managed Competition Work? *International Journal of Health Care Finance and Economics* 1 (2): 159–87.

Wilde, Louis L., and Alan Schwartz. 1979. Equilibrium Comparison Shopping. *Review of Economic Studies* 46 (3): 543–53.

About the Author

Mark V. Pauly is the Bendheim Professor in the Department of Health Care Systems and professor of health care systems, insurance and risk management, and business and public policy at the Wharton School of the University of Pennsylvania. He is also a professor of economics in the School of Arts and Sciences. He is co–editor-in-chief of the *International Journal of Health Care Finance and Economics* and associate editor of the *Journal of Risk and Uncertainty*. Dr. Pauly is a former commissioner on the Physician Payment Review Commission and an active member of the Institute of Medicine, where he has served on panels on public accountability for health insurers under Medicare and improving the financing of vaccines. He is a former member of the advisory committee to the Agency for Health Care Research and Quality and the Medicare Technical Advisory Panel. He received a Ph.D. in economics from the University of Virginia.

Dr. Pauly's scholarship focuses on medical economics and health insurance. His research areas include appropriate design for Medicare in a budget-constrained environment and ways to reduce the number of uninsured through tax credits for public and private insurance. Dr. Pauly's study on the economics of moral hazard was the first to point out how health insurance coverage may affect patients' use of medical services. Subsequent work, both theoretical and empirical, has explored the impact of conventional insurance coverage on preventive care, outpatient care, and prescription drug use in managed care. Dr. Pauly has also researched the influences that determine whether insurance coverage is available and, through several cost effectiveness studies, the influence of medical care and health practices on health outcomes and cost. He is currently studying the effect of poor health on worker productivity.

Research Staff

Gerard Alexander
Visiting Scholar

Joseph Antos
Wilson H. Taylor Scholar in Health
Care and Retirement Policy

Leon Aron
Resident Scholar

Michael Auslin
Resident Scholar

Claude Barfield
Resident Scholar

Michael Barone
Resident Fellow

Roger Bate
Resident Fellow

Walter Berns
Resident Scholar

Douglas J. Besharov
Joseph J. and Violet Jacobs
Scholar in Social Welfare Studies

Andrew Biggs
Resident Fellow

Edward Blum
Visiting Fellow

Dan Blumenthal
Resident Fellow

John R. Bolton
Senior Fellow

Karlyn Bowman
Senior Fellow

Arthur C. Brooks
Visiting Scholar

Richard Burkhauser
Visiting Scholar

John E. Calfee
Resident Scholar

Charles W. Calomiris
Visiting Scholar

Lynne V. Cheney
Senior Fellow

Steven J. Davis
Visiting Scholar

Mauro De Lorenzo
Resident Fellow

Thomas Donnelly
Resident Fellow

Nicholas Eberstadt
Henry Wendt Scholar in Political
Economy

Mark Falcoff
Resident Scholar Emeritus

John C. Fortier
Research Fellow

Ted Frank
Resident Fellow; Director,
AEI Legal Center for the
Public Interest

David Frum
Resident Fellow

David Gelernter
National Fellow

Reuel Marc Gerecht
Resident Fellow

Newt Gingrich
Senior Fellow

James K. Glassman
Senior Fellow; Editor-in-Chief,
The American magazine

Jack L. Goldsmith
Visiting Scholar

Robert A. Goldwin
Resident Scholar Emeritus

Scott Gottlieb, M.D.
Resident Fellow

Kenneth P. Green
Resident Scholar

Michael S. Greve
John G. Searle Scholar

Christopher Griffin
Research Fellow

Robert W. Hahn
Senior Fellow; Executive Director,
AEI Center for Regulatory and
Market Studies

Kevin A. Hassett
Senior Fellow; Director,
Economic Policy Studies

Steven F. Hayward
F. K. Weyerhaeuser Fellow

Robert B. Helms
Resident Scholar

Frederick M. Hess
Resident Scholar; Director,
Education Policy Studies

Ayaan Hirsi Ali
Resident Fellow

R. Glenn Hubbard
Visiting Scholar

Frederick W. Kagan
Resident Scholar

Leon R. Kass, M.D.
Hertog Fellow

Herbert G. Klein
National Fellow

Marvin H. Kosters
Resident Scholar Emeritus

Irving Kristol
Senior Fellow Emeritus

Desmond Lachman
Resident Fellow

Michael A. Ledeen
Freedom Scholar

Adam Lerrick
Visiting Scholar

Philip I. Levy
Resident Scholar

James R. Lilley
Senior Fellow

Lawrence B. Lindsey
Visiting Scholar

John H. Makin
Visiting Scholar

N. Gregory Mankiw
Visiting Scholar

Aparna Mathur
Research Fellow

Mark B. McClellan, M.D.
Visiting Senior Fellow, Health Policy
Studies and AEI Center for
Regulatory and Market Studies

Allan H. Meltzer
Visiting Scholar

Thomas P. Miller
Resident Fellow

Joshua Muravchik
Resident Scholar

Charles Murray
W. H. Brady Scholar

Roger F. Noriega
Visiting Fellow

Michael Novak
George Frederick Jewett Scholar
in Religion, Philosophy, and
Public Policy

Norman J. Ornstein
Resident Scholar

Richard Perle
Resident Fellow

Tomas Philipson
Visiting Scholar

Alex J. Pollock
Resident Fellow

Vincent R. Reinhart
Resident Scholar

Michael Rubin
Resident Scholar

Sally Satel, M.D.
Resident Scholar

Gary J. Schmitt
Resident Scholar; Director,
Program on Advanced
Strategic Studies

David Schoenbrod
Visiting Scholar

Joel M. Schwartz
Visiting Fellow

Kent Smetters
Visiting Scholar

Christina Hoff Sommers
Resident Scholar

Samuel Thernstrom
Director, AEI Press; Director,
W. H. Brady Program

Bill Thomas
Visiting Fellow

Richard Vedder
Visiting Scholar

Alan D. Viard
Resident Scholar

Peter J. Wallison
Arthur F. Burns Fellow in
Financial Policy Studies

Ben J. Wattenberg
Senior Fellow

David A. Weisbach
Visiting Scholar

Paul Wolfowitz
Visiting Scholar

John Yoo
Visiting Scholar

DATE DUE

Demco, Inc. 38-293